A Word A Day

A Word
A Day

A Romp
through Some of the Most
Unusual and Intriguing
Words in English

Anu Garg
with Stuti Garg

This edition published 2003
by BCA
by arrangement with John Wiley & Sons, Inc.

CN 111950

First reprint 2003

Printed and bound in Germany by
GGP Media, Pößneck

Every word was once a poem.
—RALPH WALDO EMERSON

"What are you doing, Daddy?"

"I'm writing a book, Ananya."

"What kind of book?"

"It's a book of words."

"OK, can you write *cat?*"

"Well, it's supposed to be a book of big and hard words."

"OK, how about *peacock?*"

"That's fine."

"And how about *heart* and *snowflake* and *teddy bear* and *dark green* and *purple* and *telephone* and *sun*...I want to write a book too!"

Sometimes simpler words are more profound.

Contents

Acknowledgments

A number of people contributed to make this book possible. A big thank-you to all the linguaphiles on A.Word.A.Day (AWAD) for being a part of the AWAD community. We've learned much from you. Thanks to Carolanne Reynolds for reviewing drafts of the book and for her comments. Thank you to Todd Derr and Eric Shackle for their dedication to AWAD.

Thank you to Chip Rossetti, our editor, for believing in this book and for steering it to completion.

Special thanks to Bill Holland for his support.

A humble thank-you to our parents for their blessings.

A bow to our guru.

Introduction

This is a book of words. But then, all books are books of words. This book is an expression of the joy of words, the magic of words, the music of words. It's a book of words arranged in many thematic bouquets, each bouquet collecting words of a kind. Words that make us laugh, words that make us feel incredulous, words that pack a whole story in just a few letters, words that delight us, and words of many other shapes, sizes, and hues.

Perhaps it's no coincidence that the word *words* is an anagram of *sword*. Well-used words cut through ambiguity and confusion like a sharp sword in the hands of an expert swordsman. Like a fencer with a whole supply of moves, feints, and parries, a person with a large and varied vocabulary at her command can find just the right word for the occasion. Whether we realize it or not, words touch something deep within all of us, for what would we be without words? Words move us, inspire, animate, motivate, challenge, and delight us. It's what this whole book is about.

Take the word *delight,* for instance. Are we put into dark when we are "de-lighted"? Not exactly. The word *delite* might sound like a corruption of the word brought forth by some marketer, but that's the source of the word. The word *delight* came to us from earlier *delite,* which ultimately is from the same source as the word *delectable.*

1

Would you believe that *lettuce* is a cousin of *milk;* that *corduroy* literally means "the cloth of the king" (and hence the king of cloth?); that *salary* comes to us from *salt;* that *trivia* takes its origins from *crossroads;* that when you *flex* your muscles, you are "moving mice," etymologically speaking; that *cockamamie* draws inspiration from fake tattoos; that *carnival* rose from the idea of taking meat away during Lent; that *cynic* has its origins in *canines.* Countless other words have similarly surprising derivations. That's the marvel of words, leading us to unexpected corners waiting to be discovered.

Then there is arrangement of letters. Not one or two, but dozens of words have all five vowels in them. And there are many with all five vowels in order, such as *facetious* and *abstemious,* to name two examples. There are words within words; for instance, *tiger* is inside *dentigerous* (one having teeth). And there are semordnilaps, or words that are formed by reversing other words, such as *drab* and *bard.*

Going down from words to letters, did you know that all continents begin and end with the same letter? And that all, except Europe, begin and end with the letter *A?* Isn't it interesting to know that *Q* is the only letter in the alphabet that does not appear in the name of any state of the United States?

How do you remember the difference between the two kinds of camels, dromedaries and bactrians? Easy! Notice the beginning letters: one bump in a *D,* two bumps in a *B.* When you visit a cave and marvel at nature's enchanting formations, which are stalagmites and which ones stalactites? Stala**g**mites are formed on the **g**round while stala**c**tites hang from the **c**eiling.

Open the dictionary and feast on the words. The bigger the better—an unabridged is the best—and discover that world where each word is a world in itself. Mark Twain, that master of words, once jocularly observed about a dictionary, "I have studied it often, but I never could discover the plot." Well, a dictionary is a place where each word has a plot, a whole history behind it. Each word has its own biography—we call it etymology. They change, they evolve, they adapt, they die, and they get revived.

Even though this book presents made-up examples, all of these words can be found in the pages of popular newspapers, magazines, books, and web sites—though not that often. That's to say that these are *real* words, not obscure words picked from a word museum. I hope you enjoy them. You're invited to join my daily romp through the world of words. You can subscribe to A. Word. A. Day (AWAD) at http://wordsmith.org. I look forward to your comments and suggestions about the experiences of words at anu@wordsmith.org.

Welcome to the world of words!

CHAPTER 1

Animal Words

It's a blessing to have a child at home. As a parent, I strive to answer my daughter Ananya's incessant questions about the moon and earthworms and clouds and trees and bears as truthfully as I can. Our investigations into these seemingly mundane matters often reveal insights that are learning experiences for both of us. But there are times when my thoughts are elsewhere and I simply answer the question "Why?" with, "Because that's how God made them." I didn't know the joke was on me until the evening I found the corner of our living room wall scribbled with bright shades of crayons. When questioned why we had that mural on the wall, she simply replied, "Because that's how God made it."

Well, if we were to ask why a crab moves crabwise or sideways, that'd be a pretty good answer: Because that's how God (or nature, depending on how your beliefs run) made crabs. Because that's how their legs bend. That's how their muscles flex. That's how they've adapted. That's how they survive as a species. And that's how we got a synonym for the word *sideways* in our dictionary. If we were to look up the term *humanwise* in a crab's dictionary, chances are it would mean *sideways*.

Here are a few words derived from animals (the only animal-based products we use around here).

crabwise (KRAB-wyz)
adjective   1. Sideways. 2. In a cautious or roundabout manner.
From the sideways movement of crabs. Also see *cancrine* (chapter 31).

● And then in a true action–film manner, the hero began moving
  crabwise along the wall while scanning the alley for the villain.

testudinate (te-STOOD-in-ayt), also **testudinal** or
testudinarian
adjective   1. Slow-moving, like a turtle. 2. Curved like the cara-
pace (shell) of a turtle; vaulted.
noun   A turtle.
From Late Latin *testudinatus*, from Latin *testudo* (tortoise).

● "I kinda find his slow pace and curved back alluring," the
  young fashion model fawned about the *testudinate* geriatric
  who just happened to be an oil magnate as well.

Test U Do?

In ancient Rome, on certain occasions when the legionar-
ies were under attack, they would clump together and hold
their shields outward, with the central men holding their
shields above their heads. In this way the shields acted like a
shell around the cohort, and the name of this formation
was *testudo*.

—*Julie Murdoch, South Perth, Australia*

---

gadfly (GAD-fly)
noun   1. One who persistently annoys or one who prods into action. 2. Any of the various types of flies that bite livestock.

• • •

Philosophy is a battle against the bewitchment of our intelligence
by means of language.
—LUDWIG WITTGENSTEIN, philosopher (1889–1951)

From *gad* (a goad for cattle), from Middle English, from Old Norse *gaddr*.

● The newspaper columnist saw himself as a public *gadfly,* keeping politicians honest and running critical articles about them when they weren't.

kangaroo court (kang-guh-ROO kort)

noun   A mock court set up with disregard to proper procedure to deliver a judgment arrived at in advance.

From the Old West to the Spanish Inquisition to the Salem Witch Trials, kangaroo courts have made their appearances throughout history. While theories abound regarding the origin of this expression, lexicographers haven't found a convincing proof of one or another, and its derivation can be tagged with the succinct "origin unknown." But that doesn't stop us from speculating. Some believe it comes from the animal itself—a funny-looking creature that bounces around without appearing to achieve anything. Then some think it is so named because it jumps to conclusions. According to one line of thought, the British didn't respect the Australian penal colony enough to give them due process of law, and with that legacy we name it so. Or maybe it is because this setup describes courts whose opinions wander "all over the place"—opinions that change so much from case to case that the court precedent "bounces" like this member of the marsupial family. Others surmise that the term originated from the Gold Rush era involving the trial of some Aussie miners.

● ● ●

Poetry is a deal of joy and pain and wonder,
with a dash of the dictionary.
—KAHLIL GIBRAN, mystic, poet, playwright, and artist (1883–1931)

Jumping to Conclusions

I have known, from youthful days in Tennessee, a kangaroo court to be one which sets its own rules of procedure, and more specifically one in which the plaintiff and the defendant can find themselves in switched positions with the plaintiff being found guilty and the defendant innocent, and not necessarily of the initial charge.

—*R. David Cox, Galax, Virginia*

waspish (WOS-pish)

adjective   1. Like a wasp, in behavior (stinging) or in form (slender build). 2. Easily annoyed; irascible; petulant. 3. Of or pertaining to a WASP (White Anglo Saxon Protestant).

From *wasp*, from Middle English *waspe*, from Old English *waesp*, from *waeps*.

● When she called him *waspish* in her most charming voice, the cranky, lean fellow didn't know what attribute of his she found so alluring.

• • •

He is a hard man who is only just, and a sad one who is only wise.
—Voltaire, philosopher (1694–1778)

CHAPTER 2

Latin Terms

Although a "dead" language, Latin remains alive through its extensive vocabulary, which is used in fields such as medicine, science, and law, and also via the numerous words that the English language has borrowed and built upon. And it is still the official language of the Vatican.

We use Latin expressions for many purposes, sometimes to sound more literary and at times for idioms that pack a concept in just a few words that would otherwise take a few sentences. *Quid pro quo,* for example, tells us in only three words the idea of "you scratch my back and I'll scratch yours." Here are a few terms from Latin that are often used in the English language.

Found in Translation

I recall one of my history professors telling the class about his friend who taught the Late Middle Ages and Early Modern period of Spanish history. My professor didn't know Spanish and had no great desire to learn yet another language, and his counterpart felt the same way about American English, but they quickly discovered that both knew Latin and they corresponded for thirty years in Latin! So perhaps the reports of Latin's death, like Mark Twain's, have been greatly exaggerated!

—*Rhonda L. Stroud, Seattle, Washington*

quid pro quo (KWID pro kwo), plural **quid pro quos** or **quids pro quo**

noun Something given or taken in exchange for something else.

From Latin *quid* (something) *pro* (for) *quo* (something).

● The campaign contributors knew that the members of congress are pros at *quid pro quo*.

rara avis (RAR-uh AY-vis), plural **rarae aves** (RAR-ee AY-veez)

noun A rare person or thing.

From Latin *rara* (rare) and *avis* (bird).

● As a font of jewels such as "It's time for the human race to enter the solar system" and "It's wonderful to be here in the great state of Chicago," Dan Quayle was a *rara avis*.

Newsbreak

In the earlier part of the twentieth century, in the county of Caithness in the north of Scotland, great excitement arose when a pot (or part thereof) was discovered, apparently stemming from the Roman occupation of Britain. It was exciting because there was no archaeological evidence up to that point of the Romans' having been that far north. The local newspaper, *The Caithness Courier*, gave prominence to the find, and quoted in full the inscription on the artifact. It was ITI SAPIS SPOTANDA BIGO NE. The *Courier* never lived down its naiveté.

—*Ron Gilbertson, Kingston, Ontario, Canada*

● ● ●

Life is a long lesson in humility.
—JAMES M. BARRIE, author (1860–1937)

sine die (SY-nee DY-ee, SIN-ay DEE-ay)
adverb Without designating a future day for action or meeting; indefinitely.
From Latin *sine* (without) and *die* (day).

● As the time for his golf game neared, the judge adjourned the trial *sine die.*

annus mirabilis (AN-uhs mi-RAB-uh-lis), plural **anni mirabiles** (AN-i mi-RAB-uh-leez)
noun A remarkable year.
From Latin *annus* (year) *mirabilis* (wondrous).

● Earlier in the year he lost the election for the post of president of the Pet Lizard Owners Club, during the summer his daughter ran away to join a circus, and then later in the year a rabid dog bit him in the street. It wasn't going to be exactly an *annus mirabilis,* Jim realized.

sub rosa (sub RO-zuh)
adverb Secretly, privately, or confidentially.
From Latin *sub* (under) *rosa* (rose). From the ancient practice of using a rose as a symbol of secrecy.

● The challenger in the mayoral race knew the difficulty of winning against the incumbent with such an exceptional record, so he figured it would be best to launch *sub rosa* attacks insinuating that the incumbent practiced pyromancy—making decisions by the shapes appearing in the fire.

● ● ●
Eloquence is a painting of the thoughts.
—BLAISE PASCAL, philosopher and mathematician (1623–1662)

Who Says Latin Is Dead?

Here are a few Latin terms for modern times that you can use for fun and profit:

Prescriptio in manibus tabellariorium est. (The check is in the mail.)

Purgamentum init, exit purgamentum. (Garbage in, garbage out.)

Semper ubi sub ubi. (Always wear underwear).

Die dulci fruere. (Have a nice day.)

Sona si Latine loqueris. (Honk if you speak Latin.)

Fac ut vivas. (Get a life.)

Cave canem. (Beware of the dog.)

Quidquid latine dictum sit, altum videtur. (Anything said in Latin sounds profound.)

* * *

Solitude is a silent storm that breaks down all our dead branches; / Yet it sends our living roots deeper into the living heart of the living earth.
—KAHLIL GIBRAN, mystic, poet, playwright, and artist (1883–1931)

CHAPTER 3

Words to Describe People I

The pejorative suffix *-aster* (meaning something that is inferior, small, or shallow) gives us some delightful words when it comes to name-calling. A reviewer brands a poet a *poetaster* (an inferior poet) and the reviewee might return the favor by calling the former a *criticaster* (an incompetent critic). In the same vein, we can have a politicaster, an astrologaster, and the bane of writers everywhere—a grammaticaster. Lest we get carried away here, let's remember that a grandmaster is not an inferior grandma. Well, enough of the pretend words. Here are some real words to describe people.

philosophaster (fi–los–uh–FAS–tuhr, fi–LOS–uh–fas–tuhr)
noun   A pseudo-philosopher.
From Late Latin, *philosopher* + *-aster,* a pejorative suffix indicating something that is inferior or mimics another.

● Here are the droll spumings of some *philosophaster* on the Internet:

Why did the chicken cross the road?

Plato: For the greater good.

Karl Marx: It was a historical inevitability.

Nietzsche: Because if you gaze too long across the road, the road gazes also across you.

Aristotle: To actualize its potential.

Ralph Waldo Emerson: It didn't cross the road; it transcended it.

Johann von Goethe: The eternal hen-principle made it do it.

Henry David Thoreau: To live deliberately . . . and suck all the marrow out of life.

autocrat (O-tuh-krat)
noun   A ruler with absolute power or a person who has unrestricted authority.
From French *autocrate,* from Greek *autokrates, auto-* (self) + *-krates, -crat* (ruling).

● "Power tends to corrupt, and absolute power corrupts absolutely." These words of historian Lord Acton succinctly explain why it's difficult to find a benign *autocrat* in history.

adamantine (ad-uh-MAN-teen, -tin)
adjective   1. Unyielding or firm. 2. Like a diamond in hardness or luster.
From Middle English, from Old French *adamaunt,* from Latin *adamas, adamant* (hard metal, steel, diamond, etc.), from Greek

• • •

Fame is a vapor; popularity an accident;
the only earthly certainty is oblivion.
—MARK TWAIN, author and humorist (1835–1910)

adamas, adamant, a- (not) + *daman* (to conquer). The word *diamond* is also derived from the same root.

● Finally, Clio figured out what would it take to overcome her *adamantine* posture—a few *adamantine* stones, the precious kind.

satrap (SAY-trap, SAT-rap)
noun   1. A governor of a province in ancient Persia. 2. A subordinate ruler or official.
From Middle English *satrape,* from Latin *satrapes,* from Greek *satrapes,* from Old Persian *khshathrapavan* (protector of the country).

● Dealing with the head of the company was easy, but her *satraps* were a different story.

anchorite (ANG-kuh-ryt), also **anchoret** (ANG-kuhr-it)
noun   One who lives in seclusion; a hermit.
From Middle English, Medieval Latin, Late Latin, Late Greek, from Greek *anakhoretes* (one who withdraws or retreats).

● And then it dawned on him. In order to survive in this world, you have to deal with people who are less than perfect, unless you wish to live like an *anchorite* on some mountain.

● ● ●

We are all born originals—why is it so many of us die copies?
—EDWARD YOUNG, poet (1683–1765)

CHAPTER 4

Lesser-Known Counterparts of Everyday Words

Author and humorist Mark Twain once observed, "The difference between the right word and the almost right word is the difference between lightning and a lightning bug." Open a newspaper or magazine and chances are you'll read about the frightening "epidemic" of mad cow disease. Of course, it is we who are mad when we feed these herbivore animals body parts of other animals, including other cows, but I digress. With the word *epizootic,* we know the right term to use when it comes to an animal disease. The root *dem(os)* in the word *epidemic,* meaning "people," is the same root that gave us the word *democracy.* Here are two other words with their animal equivalents: *endemic/enzootic* and *demography/zoography.* Let's look at some other, lesser-known counterparts of everyday words.

epizootic (ep-uh-zo-OT-ik)
adjective   Spreading quickly among many animals.

noun   Such a disease.

From French *epizootique,* from *epi-* + Greek *zoion* (animal).

● Nor can today's oldest oldster recall the "great *epizootic*" of 1872. This was a flulike disease that killed at least 20,000 horse-car horses in the nation. When the *epizootic* quit killing horses, inventive Americans sought new pulling power.
> —*Jack Goodman, discussing trolley cars of a bygone era,*
> *in the* Salt Lake Tribune *(June 27, 1999)*

anile (AN-yl, AY-nyl)

adjective   Of or like an old woman.

From Latin *anilis,* from *anus* (old woman). *Senile* is the male equivalent of this word.

● Why is it that juvenile and *anile* get along so well? Because they have a common enemy: mother.

estivate (ES-tuh-vayt), also aestivate

verb   To pass the summer in a dormant state.

From Latin *aestivatus,* past participle of *aestivare* (to reside during the summer).

Hibernate is the winter equivalent of this word.

● Pertheus, having bought the Internet stock at low cost, was dreaming of quitting the job and *estivating.* Ah, if only things always went up.

● ● ●

Life is all memory, except for the one present moment that goes by
so quick you hardly catch it going.
—TENNESSEE WILLIAMS, playwright (1911–1983)

At Least They Are Not Restive-ate

The word *estivate* struck a nerve—a deep, deep nerve—
with me. Anyone wishing to see the ultimate example is invited to visit my home this summer and observe the
teenage boy who *estivates* there.

—*Jennie Burden, Manhattan, Kansas*

---

thegosis (THEE-go-sis)
noun　Grinding of teeth as a means of sharpening them.
From Greek *thegos* (to sharpen). *Bruxism* is the word for "night-
time grinding of teeth."

● While others enjoyed the after-dinner conversation, it was
Uncle Verdi's favorite time to engage in the daily *thegosis* to be
ready to attack the next day's meals.

trilemma (tri-LEM-uh)
noun　A situation offering three undesirable options.
Blend of *tri-* + *dilemma*.

● The dish wasn't proving very agreeable to Bertrand's stomach
and he faced a *trilemma:* tell his host that the preparation was
unpalatable and face her wrath, feign that it was delicious and
risk being offered more, or pretend that he was feeling sick to
avoid eating it and be forced to take her homemade medicine
instead.

• • •

The best and most beautiful things in the world cannot be seen or even
touched. They must be felt with the heart.
—HELEN KELLER, author and speaker (1880–1968)

Give Them Dictionaries, Take Away Their Guns

Trilemma reminds me of an infamous mathematical problem called "The Truel" (as opposed to duel). In that problem you're facing two other competitors, and you all have guns. Each of you is allowed to fire one shot at a time. Unfortunately, you're the worst shooter of the three, hitting the target only once in every three tries. The others hit every second shot and every shot, respectively. The shooting takes place in order of ability to shoot, starting with the weakest. So, you have the first shot. What should you do to maximize your chances to stay alive? Should you aim for the guy who hits once every second shot or aim for the guy who hits every time?

To make a long story short, you do neither. Your best option is to fire your shot in the air, and let the other two guys deal with themselves. Firing the shot in the air forces the next person to aim at the guy who always hits. If he hits, great, then you have the next shot; if he misses, then the "always-hitter" will aim at the "50-percent guy" because that guy is his worst enemy. In either case, you're still alive after the first round, and you have only one person to deal with. Your chances still aren't that great, but they're better than trying to kill somebody during the first round (which means that it's highly likely that one of the guys will be alive to kill you after the first round is over).

—*Kai Holthaus, Los Gatos, California*

• • •

With time and patience the mulberry leaf becomes a silk gown.
—CHINESE PROVERB

CHAPTER 5

Words for Odds and Ends

The Internet is overloaded. I'm told its wires are clogged with pirated song clips, fuzzy videos, and dirty pictures. I think the real reason behind the congestion is that confounded "angry, hungry, -gry" puzzle that has been known to make the rounds of the Internet googols of times. It shows up in my mailbox with unfailing regularity.

Unlike that *-gry* chestnut, I do like to see word-related queries. This collection of words attempts to answer some of those and focuses on questions of the type, "Do you know the word for that metal thingy at the end of a shoestring?" So let's look at words for things we see around us every day but don't know what they are called.

aglet (AG-let)
noun　A tag at the end of a lace or cord to prevent it from getting frazzled and to help in passing it through an eyelet.
The word for this seemingly insignificant thingy comes to us from Latin *acus* (needle or pin) via French. In French, an *aiguille* is a needle, so *aiguillette* is, literally, a little needle.

● Kelly figured that specialization was the wave of the future, and following in the footsteps of her father, Al Bundy, the shoe man, she decided to launch a store selling only shoelaces tipped with designer *aglets*.

chad (chad)

noun   A small piece of paper generated from punching holes in a paper.

We can credit the 2000 U.S. presidential election with making this a household word. If there were any doubt that a little piece of paper could change the course of history, *chad* removes it unequivocally. Yet, the origins of this word are lost in history. According to popular yet unsubstantiated theories, we got it from corruption of *chaff,* from Hindi *chheda* (hole), or from the name of an inventor called Chadless who designed a punching machine that didn't produce these tiny circles. His machine made holes but didn't remove the pieces all the way and let them hang on to the mother paper, thus eliminating confetti mess on the floor. If the chadless punch didn't produce these bits of paper, they must be called *chad,* so the logic goes. Some claim *chad* to be an acronym with a fanciful derivation: **C**ard **H**ole **A**gglomerate **D**ebris.

● Always an idea person, Joubert received the first prize from Acme Computer Paper Corporation for his suggestion of selling *chad* as packaged confetti.

● ● ●

When love and skill work together, expect a masterpiece.
—JOHN RUSKIN, author, art critic, and social reformer (1819–1900)

Kinds of Chad

Ones that count:

- hanging door—one corner hanging off
- swinging door—two corners hanging off
- tri-chad—three corners hanging off

Ones that don't:

- pregnant—bulges, but not punched through (leading to a *miscarriage* of justice)
- dimple—simple indentation

tittle (TIT-tl)

noun   1. A dot on top of the letter *i* or other mark used in writing and printing, such as a diacritic accent mark. 2. A small amount of something. Used in idiom "jot or tittle": a little amount. From Latin *titulus* (superscription, title).

Other words derived from the same root include *tilde, title,* and *entitle.*

● When she lost the title of the estate owing to a missing *tittle* in her deceased uncle's will, Edna realized the importance of dotting one's *i*'s and crossing one's *t*'s.

grommet (GROM-it), also grummet (GRUM-)

noun   A metal or plastic ring to reinforce an eyelet.

A *grommet* is to an eyelet what an aglet is to a lace. This word is also variously used to refer to similar objects in many fields. For example, a washer to insulate a hole, a ring, or a loop to fasten the edge of a sail to its stay.

• • •

The barriers are not erected which can say to aspiring talents and industry, "Thus far and no farther."
—LUDWIG VAN BEETHOVEN, composer (1770–1827)

- Even though he accepted the job of feeding guinea pigs at night in a research lab, Sylk, an aspiring rock star, felt he was going to be a square *grommet* in a round eyelet.

pintle (PIN-tl)
noun   A bolt or pin on which another part turns.
Can you guess the origin of this innocuous-sounding term? It comes from Old English via Middle English *pintel* (penis).

- For want of a *pintle* the whole kingdom was lost.

• • •

Honest differences are often a healthy sign of progress.
—MAHATMA GANDHI, leader and social reformer (1869–1948)

CHAPTER 6

Reduplicatives

It's time for "The Reduplicatives." That could be the name of a rock band—the one known for *razzle-dazzle* and their *hoity-toity* demeanor. They come in pairs, make a little *chit-chat,* and then *hurry-scurry* off to their next gig. Reduplicatives are words formed when a term is either repeated exactly as it is (as in *bonbon*), or with a slight variation in the vowel (as in *Ping-Pong*) or consonant (as in *higgledy-piggledy*). This process of compound word formation is known as reduplication.

So let's not *shilly-shally* or be *wishy-washy,* let's look at the *mish-mash* of a few such *super-duper* words.

shilly-shally (SHIL–ee-shal-ee)
verb intr.   To procrastinate, hesitate, or vacillate.
noun   Indecision, vacillation.
adverb   In an hesitant or irresolute manner.
adjective   Vacillating. Exhibiting a lack of decisiveness.
From reduplication of the term "Shall I?"

● Herman *shilly-shallied* too long on whether to marry Wanda or Rama, and he was left to spend his life with his three black cats and a blind chihuahua.

tussie-mussie (TUS-ee-MUS-ee) or **tuzzy-muzzy**
(TUZ-ee-MUZ-ee)
noun   A bunch of flowers; a bouquet, nosegay, garland, or posy.
From Middle English *tussemose,* apparently reduplication of *tusse* (a bunch of flowers).

● While many thought Aunt Bertha had let the weeds grow around her house owing to sheer laziness, few knew she had been saving them for a special design she had in mind for the annual *tussie-mussie* contest.

herky-jerky (HUR-kee-JUR-kee)
adjective   Moving in a sudden, spasmodic, irregular way.
From reduplication of *jerky.*

● The director was at a loss to understand why his movie missed an award at the Sundance Film Festival, even though he had tried his best to turn it into an art movie by shooting its full three and a half hours in *herky-jerky* frames.

wishy-washy (WISH-ee-wosh-ee)
adjective   1. Lacking in decisiveness, determination, or purpose.
2. Watery; lacking in strength, flavor, or taste.
From reduplication of *washy* (watery). A descriptive synonym of this phrase is milk-and-water.

● Unable to decide whether to send a peace delegation to the dictator or drop a bomb on him, the *wishy-washy* president chose to toss a coin.

● ● ●

It is as hard for the good to suspect evil, as it is for the bad to suspect good.
—MARCUS TULLIUS CICERO, statesman,
orator, and writer (106–43 B.C.E.)

knick-knack, also **nick-nack** (NIK-nak)
noun   A piece of ornamental article; trinket; gew-gaw; a part of bric-a-brac.
From reduplication of *knack* (toy).

● Countless *knick-knacks* and books based on the princess's life were eagerly devoured by the celebrity-hungry public, and the retailers quietly dubbed her the Princess of Sales.

• • •

As scarce as truth is, the supply has always been in excess of the demand.
—JOSH BILLINGS, humorist (1818–1885)

CHAPTER 7

Discover
the Theme I

It is human nature to find patterns in things where there might be none, whether it is in the shape of clouds or in the arrangement of sand, in a chain of events, or in the digits of pi. Or in a list of words. What unites these words here in a common thread? You'll find out! Don your word-sleuth hat and discover the theme that weaves these words. Each word is another piece of the puzzle. The answer is on page 193.

tessera (TESS-er-a), plural **tesserae**
noun   A small piece of stone, glass, etc. used in making a mosaic pattern.
This word comes to us from Greek *tesseres,* meaning "four," as in the four corners of a piece used to create a mosaic pattern. From Latin, from Greek, neuter of *tesseres,* variant of *tessares* (four).

- The kings delighted in playing chess on a giant checkerboard made of thousands of black and white *tesserae,* with live animals and people dressed as chess pieces standing on it for hours.

hypolimnion (hip-o-LIMN-ee-on)
noun   The lower layer of water in a lake that is stagnant and remains at a constant temperature.
From Greek *hypo-* (under) + *limnion,* diminutive of *limne* (lake, pool).

● The cruise ship *Sultanic* hit the iceberg, and soon it was resting among the *hypolimnion* layers of the lake.

decerebrate (de-CER-uh-brayt)
verb   To remove the cerebrum.
noun   One who is devoid of intelligence or reason.
From Latin *cerebrum* (brain).

● When Dr. Braegen *decerebrated* his third patient in a botched brain operation, his surgery privileges were taken away, and his practice was limited to treating toenail fungus.

homonym (HOM-uh-nim)
noun   A word that is the same in spelling and pronunciation as another word but different in meaning. For example, *quail* (the bird) and *quail* (to lose heart).
From Latin *homonymum,* from Greek *homonumon,* from neuter of *homonumos* (homonymous).

● When the animal refused to come out of the cage in the middle of the circus, the animal trainer didn't miss the opportunity to make wordplay with *homonyms,* "Please bear with me while I get the bear out."

• • •

Music washes away from the soul the dust of everyday life.
—BERTHOLD AUERBACH, author (1812–1882)

extravasate (ik-STRAV-uh-sayt)

verb tr.   To force to come out of a vessel, such as blood from blood vessels to surrounding tissues or lava from underground.

verb intr.   To pour forth.

From Latin combining form *extra-* (outside, beyond) + *vas* (vessel) + *-ate.*

● Unhappy at his wife's complaints that he squeezed the tube in the middle, Johann bought a rolling pin to *extravasate* the last remaining atoms of the toothpaste out.

. . .

I am beginning to learn that it is the sweet, simple things of life
which are the real ones after all.
—Laura Ingalls Wilder, author (1867–1957)

CHAPTER 8

Gender-Specific Nouns

When was the last time you came across a victrix, an authoress, an usherette, or a comedienne? As you might have already figured, these are now-obsolete feminine forms of the nouns *victor, author, usher,* and *comedian,* formed by appending the suffixes *-trix, -ess, -ette,* and *-enne,* respectively.

Many believe these gender-specific words connote inferiority *(leather/leatherette),* diminutive size *(novel/novelette),* or lesser social status *(governor/governess),* and they prefer that the same term be applied to both males and females, especially when the sex of the person is immaterial in context. As a result, especially in the U.S., the word *actor* is preferred for both men and women, *chairman* is giving way to *chair,* and *firemen/firewomen* are becoming *firefighters,* to cite but three examples.

This development may be a relief for modern schoolchildren who no longer have to remember whether they should use *aviatrix, aviatress,* or *aviatorette* when writing an essay about women flying aircraft. Things are not always that easy, however. There are still places where one needs to know separate terms for male and female forms. Here are some terms that are gender-specific and without a suffix-enabled counterpart.

caryatid (kar-ee-AT-id), plural **caryatids** or **caryatides**
    (-i-deez)
noun   A column in the shape of a female figure.
From Latin *caryatides,* plural of *caryatis,* from Greek *karyatides*
(columns in the shape of women), literally "women of Karyai," a
village of Laconia in Greece.

●   Sheba had the bright idea of earning a livelihood by posing
    still as a *caryatid* in the Paris tourist spots. Her plans didn't go
    exactly as she had thought, however, when a bout of allergy
    forced her to scratch herself nonstop.

telamon (TEL-uh-mon), plural **telamones** (-MOH-neez)
noun   A sculpture of a man used as a supporting column.
From Latin *telamon,* from Greek *telamon* (bearer or support). A
synonym of this word, also from Greek mythology, is *atlas.* The
word *atlas* is derived from Atlas, a titan forced to hold the heavens.

●   Bert had to rethink his ambition to be a Broadway star when
    the first role he was assigned was not only a nonspeaking part
    but also a nonmoving one—that of a *telamon*—in a three-hour
    Greek play.

gynarchy (JIN-ar-kee, JYE-nar-, GYE-)
noun   Government by women.
From Greek *gyn-* (woman) + *-archy* (rule).
    Here are a few terms synonymous with this word: *gynecocracy,*
its variant, *gynocracy,* and *matriarchy.*

●   With four teenage daughters and a wife running the house,
    Andy often felt as if he were living in a *gynarchy.*

● ● ●
We must believe in luck.
For how else can we explain the success of those we don't like?
—JEAN COCTEAU, author and painter (1889–1963)

androcracy (an-DROK-ruh-see)
noun   Government by men.
From Greek *andro-* (male) + *-cracy* (rule).

● When asked about her goal in life, the six-year-old Gyna con-
fidently answered, "To become the president and end the *an-
drocracy* in our country."

nymphomania (nim-fuh-MAY-nee-uh, -MAYN-yuh)
noun   Excessive sexual desire in a female.
After New Latin, from Greek *nympho-* + *-mania* (excessive desire).

● Tommy had just turned fifteen, and his raging hormones were
apparent in his dreams of getting washed up on a deserted
island with a girl afflicted with *nymphomania*.

satyriasis (say-tuh-RI-uh-sis, sat-uh-)
noun   Excessive sexual desire in a male.
After New Latin, from Greek *satyr* (a mythological creature often
portrayed chasing after nymphs) + *-mania* (excessive desire).
   Also known as "Don Juanism" after the legendary fourteenth-
century Spanish nobleman.

● Cold bath, vigorous exercise, and ice packs—nothing helped
MacDum's *satyriasis* until the physician discovered his reading
preferences and prescribed him to read nothing but government memos, annual reports, and metaphysics books.

●   ●   ●

Minds, like bodies, will often fall into a pimpled, ill-conditioned state
from mere excess of comfort.
—CHARLES DICKENS, author (1812–1870)

CHAPTER 9

Verbs

They've a temper, some of them—particularly verbs, they're the proudest—adjectives you can do anything with, but not verbs—however, I can manage the whole lot of them!" boasts Humpty-Dumpty in Lewis Carroll's 1872 classic, *Through the Looking-Glass.* If they are in fact as conceited as Humpty-Dumpty claims them to be, perhaps verbs can be forgiven for their hoity-toity ways—after all, they are the ones that bring a sentence to life. How many of these verbs can you manage?

cogitate (KOJ-i-tayt)
verb tr, intr.   To ponder; meditate; think deeply.
From Latin *cogitatus,* past participle of *cogitare* (to think), from *co-* + *agitare* (to agitate, drive).

- The man who would one day *cogitate* to unravel mysteries of time and space was once described as Dull Al by his teacher. Perhaps the teacher was not far off, for as Longfellow once said, "Men of genius are often dull and inert in society; as the blazing meteor, when it descends to earth, is only a stone."

decoct (di-KOKT)

verb tr.   To extract the flavor or essence of something by boiling it.
From Middle English *decocten,* to boil, from Latin *decoquere, de-* +
coquere (to boil).

● Little Danny was ecstatic on discovering the recipe for achiev-
ing see-through vision in the latest Perry Hotter book. When
all he could achieve was a face full of pimples after *decocting* a
half-dozen herbs and drinking the resulting potion, he begged
his lawyer father to file a product liability suit against Hotter.

perorate (PER-uh-rayt)

verb intr.   1. To speak at length in a pompous way. 2. To conclude
a speech by summarizing it.
From Latin *peroratus,* past participle of *perorare,* from *per-* (through)
+ *orare* (speak).

● In the third quarter, the earnings at Prolix, Inc., showed a 37
percent decline, thanks in large part to the company CEO's
habit of *perorating* at staff meetings that kept employees away
from work.

shamble (SHAM-buhl)

verb intr.   To walk awkwardly, for example, with feet dragging or
shuffling.
Uncertain origin. Perhaps from the expression "shamble-legs"
(straddling; one walking wide) from Latin *scamnum* (butcher's
table, with rickety legs).

● When Burt's mother saw him *shambling* toward the house, she
knew—without having to look at the report card—how he
had done on his calculus exam.

• • •

Never lend books—nobody ever returns them; the only books
I have in my library are those which people have lent me.
—ANATOLE FRANCE, author and Nobel laureate (1844–1924)

redact (ri-DAKT)

verb tr. 1. To revise or edit a document for publication. 2. To compose a document.

From Middle English, from Latin *redactus,* past participle of *redigere,* from *red-* + *-actus,* past participle of *agere* (to drive or lead).

● Jon was able to get the document from the government archives but in a highly *redacted* form: all he could read that was not blacked out were words such as *the, is, to,* and *for.*

● ● ●

The artist brings something into the world that didn't exist before, and he does it without destroying something else.
—JOHN UPDIKE, author (1932–)

CHAPTER 10

Coined Words I

"My seven-year-old coined this word. Could you tell me how I can get it into a dictionary?" Questions like this pop up in my mailbox from time to time, from folks wondering how to get a word to take up residence amid the hallowed leaves of a lexicon. Thousands of new words do enter the dictionaries every year. So, what is the criterion behind their inclusion? What does a word have to do to be worthy of being called "legitimate"? Who decides what gets in and what is left out?

Usage is the single most important factor to determine if a word gains membership in that exclusive club. It has to appear extensively, over several years, in many different sources, such as newspapers, magazines, books, TV, radio, or the Internet, to show that it is gaining currency. It has to fill a need and describe a phenomenon for which no other word exists. Also, it doesn't hurt if the word is catchy and captures public imagination. The way to make it into the dictionary is to use the word often in books, magazines, and other media, and encourage other people to use it. Promote its usage—writing to dictionary publishers won't help. Although sometimes all you have to do is be the nephew of the right person (see below).

Dictionary editors read a wide variety of sources to monitor the language. They take notes—known as citations—on little

3×5 index cards or in a computer database. Once there is enough evidence, they consider whether to include it in the next edition of their dictionary, and if the answer is yes, they work to define it precisely. In this chapter, we look at coined words that have entered the dictionary.

googol (GOO-gol)

noun A number equal to 1 followed by 100 zeros (10^{100}).
Coined by Milton Sirota, nine-year-old nephew of mathematician Edward Kasner (1878–1955).

 When his little son asked how many stars there are in the universe, the mathematician Sarl Cagan explained, "*Googols* and *googols!*"

There is another number derived from *googol: googolplex*. It is equal to the number 1 followed by googol zeros.

blurb (blurb)

noun A brief description or review, especially one on a book jacket.
Coined by Frank Gelett Burgess, humorist and illustrator (1866–1951).

The original blurb was a fictional Miss Blinda Blurb, whom Gelett Burgess drew for the jacket of his book *Are You Bromide?* This voluptuous young lady was accompanied by overblown testimonials Burgess concocted for presenting his book at a book-sellers' convention. Over time all such pictures of pulchritudinous women were known as "blurbs," but today the term refers to gushing praise often found on the dust jackets. Here is how the term is defined in *Burgess Unabridged* (1914):

• • •

If you bungle raising your children,
I don't think whatever else you do well matters very much.
—JACQUELINE KENNEDY ONASSIS, former first lady (1929–1994)

Blurb 1. A flamboyant advertisement; an inspired testimonial. 2. Fulsome praise; a sound like a publisher ... On the "jacket" of the "latest" fiction, we find the blurb; abounding in agile adjectives and adverbs, attesting that this book is the "sensation of the year."

Besides the word blurb, Burgess is best remembered for his quatrain "Purple Cow":

> I never saw a purple cow
> I never hope to see one
> But I can tell you anyhow
> I'd rather see than be one.

● While the advance review of the novel said "Highly recommended to be left in bookstore," the *blurb* on the back cover of the book quoted only the phrase, "Highly recommended."

boondoggle (BOON-dog-uhl)

noun 1. A braided cord worn by Boy Scouts. 2. A wasteful activity, especially one funded by government as a political reward.
Coined by Robert H. Link, a scoutmaster. The origins of the term in the sense of a work of little value are uncertain. Perhaps it came to us from cowboys who wove braids of leather strips during lonely times on the ranch. In 1935, New Deal projects to make work were often criticized as boondoggles.

● Congressman W. Astrel was ecstatic to hear that his pet *boondoggle*—a $1.5 billion project to harness moonlight into energy—was approved by the Senate.

heebie-jeebies (HEE-bee-JEE-beez)

noun   A feeling of nervousness; jitters; creeps.

· · ·

What is called discretion in men is called cunning in animals.
—JEAN DE LA FONTAINE, poet and fabulist (1621–1695)

Coined by cartoonist Billy De Beck (1890–1942) in his comic strip *Barney Google*. Another coinage by De Beck that has found a place in the English language dictionary is *hotsy-totsy* or *hotsie-totsie*, meaning "just right" or "perfect."

● Big Al was having the *heebie-jeebies* the night before his scheduled bungee jump and decided to listen to a tape of *Barney* songs to soothe himself.

runcible (RUN-si-buhl)

noun   A combination of fork, spoon, and sometimes knife. Having three prongs with a spoonlike receptacle and a sharp edge for cutting. Also known as *spork* (a blend of *spoon* and *fork*).
Coined by Edward Lear (1812–1888), humorous verse writer and painter.

Here is the verse from the popular children's poem "The Owl and the Pussycat" by Edward Lear, in which he coined this word in 1871:

They dined on mince and slices of quince
Which they ate with a runcible spoon
And hand in hand at the edge of the sand
They danced to the light of the moon
The moon, the moon,
They danced to the light of the moon.

● When asked for a fork, the ever-efficient Lora replied, "Why, you have the *runcible* on your plate, the three-in-one thing."

. . .
If the camel once gets his nose in a tent, his body will soon follow.
—ARABIAN PROVERB

CHAPTER 11

Back-Formations

Swindle, donate, and *brainwash.* Can there be anything common among these three? What unites these verb forms in a single thread is that all of them are coined by a process known as back-formation. It is a reverse process whereby words are formed by subtraction of an affix. Thus, the previously mentioned verbs were derived from the nouns *swindler, donation,* and *brainwashing,* respectively (unlike, for example, the usual way nouns are created, e.g., *lover* from the verb *love*).

Back-formations are often the result of erroneous usage. In Middle English, the original word for *pea* was *pease.* It was mistakenly considered a plural and thus people started using the supposedly singular form *pea.* Since then, instead of the usual pease soup, we have been slurping pea soup. Let's look at five more back-formations.

emote (I-MOAT)
verb   To display emotions, especially in a theatrical or exaggerated manner.
Back-formation from *emotion.*

- Apparently Leroy was quite realistic as he *emoted* his travails in bicycling to high school, and his doctor dad soon bought him a brand new car.

admix (ad-MIKS)
verb tr., intr.   To add or mix to something.
Back-formation from obsolete *admix,* from Middle English, from Latin *admixtus.*

- Aunt Trivalia was puzzled as to why her cookies tasted a bit too sweet when she had *admixed* five cups of sugar to two cups of flour just as directed in the recipe. Unfortunately, she was oblivious to the point in ".5 cups sugar" owing to her failing eyesight.

aesthete (ES-theet, EES-), also **esthete**
noun   A person who has or pretends high sensitivity to beauty, as in art or nature.
Back-formation from *aesthetic.*

- Always an *aesthete,* Broushard was proud of having acquired the unique ancient Roman sculpture at an auction for only $3,400 on eBay, not realizing that it was a hastily patched collection of broken sanitary pipes.

adulate (AJ-uh-layt)
verb tr.   To show excessive admiration to someone.
Back-formation from *adulation,* from Middle English, from Middle French, from Latin *adulatus,* past participle of *adulare* (to fawn upon).

• • •

Superfluous wealth can buy superfluities only.
—HENRY DAVID THOREAU, naturalist and author (1817–1862)

● The sales of Superman costumes shot through the roof after the actor playing the part endorsed them in front of millions of viewers who *adulated* him.

accrete (uh-KREET)

verb tr.   To add in order to make bigger, accumulate.
verb intr.   To grow together; join.
Back-formation from *accretion*.

● Soon Herman's daily journal was gaining size, *accreting* mundane details such as taking the trash out, clearing the wrinkles on the tablecloth, and cleaning his fingernails.

• • •

They that can give up essential liberty to obtain a little temporary safety
deserve neither liberty nor safety.
—BENJAMIN FRANKLIN, statesman, author, and inventor (1706–1790)

CHAPTER 12

Portmanteaux

There are many ways words are formed. One of these is when words are coined by the fusion of two separate words. What is unique about these words, as opposed to words formed by simply placing two words next to each other (e.g., *lovesick*), is that the former are blended together in such a way that each of the participating words contributes a fragment of its whole, both in letters and in meaning to the new word. Such an amalgamated word is known as a *portmanteau* (a bag to carry clothes, typically one that opens into two halves) since Lewis Carroll gave them this moniker in his 1872 classic, *Through the Looking-Glass.*

Coincidentally, the word *portmanteau* is itself a portmanteau from the two French words, *porte-* (carry) and *manteau* (cloak).

Carroll himself coined some great portmanteaux such as *chortle* (*chuckle* + *snort*), and *slithy* (*slimy* + *lithe*).

cremains (kri-MAYNZ)
noun   The ashes of a cremated body.
Blend of *cremate* and *remains.*

- Phoebe couldn't bear the thought of parting with her bonsai collection and instructed that after she died, her *cremains* be spread among the roots of the bonsai trees.

cinematheque (sin-uh-muh-TEK)
noun   A small movie theater specializing in artistic, experimental, or classic movies.
From French, blend of *cinema* and *bibliothèque* (library).

● Aushlia had the vague feeling that her date with football-player Dave was doomed from the beginning, even though she had convinced him to watch the movie *Kinetica: Abstraction in the Moving Image* at the local *cinematheque.*

carmine (KAHR-min, -MYN)
noun   1. A crimson or deep red color. 2. A bright red pigment obtained by crushed cochineal insects.
From French *carmin* (color), from *carmine* (pigment), from Middle Latin *carminium,* perhaps a blend of Arabic *qirmiz* (kermes) and *minium* (red lead).

● As the director shouted "Action!" the actor playing the villain pulled the trigger on his faux carbine, and soon *carmine* was splattered on the chest of the movie's hero.

birl (burl)
verb tr., intr.   1. To cause (a floating log) to spin quickly by treading upon it. 2. To spin.
Perhaps a blend of *birr* (move with whirring sound) and *whirl.*

● Luther, having mastered *birling* by years of dedicated practice in a lake behind his house, was waiting for the day when it would be a featured event in the Olympics.

• • •

Few things can help an individual more than to place responsibility on him, and to let him know that you trust him.
—BOOKER T. WASHINGTON, reformer, educator, and author (1856–1915)

CHAPTER 13

Short Words

Has it ever happened to you that a short quotation you read somewhere made you think more than you would have by spending several weeks with a heavy tome? Perhaps that's what Friedrich Nietzsche had in mind when he said, "It is my ambition to say in ten sentences what others say in a whole book." In that spirit, here are a few single-syllable words, short yet potent.

vim (vim)
noun   Lively spirit; energy; enthusiasm.
From Latin, accusative of *vis* (strength, power).

- Uncle Rony could hardly wait to go to the neighborhood drugstore when he read the ad for the latest supplement, made from raccoon cartilage and crabapple root, that promised to fill him with *vim.*

fey (fay)
adjective   1. Fated to die. 2. Supernatural; clairvoyant. 3. Unusual.
From Middle English *feye,* from Old English *faege* (doomed).

- It appeared a bit *fey* to Claire that her instant camera produced only photos of her long-dead husband no matter where she focused. She was unaware that her camera was doctored by her nephew as part of his latest shenanigans.

gest (jest), also geste

noun   1. An adventurous tale. 2. A romance.
From Middle English, from Old French, from Latin *gesta* (actions).

Despite this word's medieval associations, it might be best known to modern readers in its variant spelling, as part of P. C. Wren's 1924 novel *Beau Geste,* which chronicles the adventures of soldiers in the French Foreign Legion in the Sahara desert.

● With his amusing tendency to exaggerate the excitement in his life, Waldo could make his description of a mundane trip to the store sound like a modern-day *gest.*

dun (dun)

verb tr.   To make repeated demands for repayment of a debt.
noun   1. One who makes insistent demand for payment. 2. A request for making payment. 3. Grayish-brown color.
adjective   Dull; dark; grayish brown.
Of unknown origin.

● Jouffard finally decided to close his neighborhood store and concentrate on writing based on his fifty-seven years' experience in running a business. His first book was titled *The Art of Writing* Dunning *Letters,* a tome of wisdom acquired in collecting money from his non-paying customers.

maw (maw)

noun   1. Mouth, throat, or gullet of an animal. 2. A large opening.

●   ●   ●
Be the change you want to see in the world.
—MAHATMA GANDHI, leader and social reformer (1869–1948)

From Middle English *mawe,* from Old English *maga.*

● Mother feared the sight of Uncle Theseus around dinnertime, knowing well how her laborious preparations could disappear into his unfathomable *maw* in no time.

• • •

Won't you come into the garden? I would like my roses to see you.
—RICHARD BRINSLEY SHERIDAN, playwright (1751–1816)

CHAPTER 14

Words That Make the Spell-Checker Ineffective

E ven though it can be caught by any run-of-the-mill spell-checker, *definately* is perhaps one of the most commonly misspelled words around. A quick trip to the Google search engine confirms some one million places where this spelling has been used on the Internet, on web sites, and in Usenet discussion groups. If this trend continues, maybe someday it will tiptoe its way to the dictionary as *miniscule* did: first tagged as erroneous and over time simply as a variant of *minuscule*. The word *minuscule* is derived from *minus,* not from *mini* as some thought and spelled accordingly. The word *definitely* follows the same trend due to its pronunciation.

On the other hand there are words that may appear as typos and trip a spell-checker even though they are genuine dictionary words. Here we explore few words that make our spell-checkers ineffective.

impassible (im-PAS-uh-buhl)
adjective   1. Insusceptible to pain or suffering. 2. Unfeeling, incapable of feeling emotions.
From Middle English, from Late Latin *impassibilis.*

● The pupils were amazed to see the stoic yogi remain *impassible* when a raccoon bit him in the toe. They didn't know he had spent his last fourteen years doing tapasya in a cave in the Himalayas.

wether (WETH-uhr)
noun   A castrated ram or billy goat.
From Middle English, from Old English.

● On seeing the fierce wind coming from north, the shepherd wondered whether *wethers* wither in windy weather.

specie (SPEE-shee, -see)
noun   Coin.
From Latin *species* (kind, type).
   In specie means "in kind."

● When asked why he changed his field, Kamal, the biologist-turned-stocktrader, explained, "I decided to work with the *specie* instead of the species."

angary (ANG-guh-ree) also **angaria** (ang-GAR-ee-uh)
noun   The right of a belligerent to seize the property of neutrals provided a compensation is made.
From Late Latin *angaria* (service to a lord), from Greek *angareia,* from *angaros.*

● ● ●

One who condones evils is just as guilty as the one who perpetrates it.
—Dr. Martin Luther King Jr., civil rights activist (1929–1968)

- "Why did you snatch pencils from Jane, an innocent by-stander, to poke Al with during your fight with him?" the principal enquired of little Jimmy. "The right of *angary,* sir," Jimmy replied. "I gave her a chocolate later."

demur (di-MUR)
verb intr. 1. To delay, hesitate, or object. 2. To file a demurrer (a pleading in court that the facts of allegation, even if true, do not support the contention).
noun Objection, hesitation.
From Latin *demorari* (to delay), via Old French and Middle English.

- Even though Fitzgibbon faintly *demurred* in the beginning when his name was proposed for president of the AOL CD Collector's Club, he was pleased to be elected to the exalted post.

· · ·
The willing contemplation of vice is vice.
—ARABIC PROVERB

CHAPTER 15

Names
for Things

As a parent of a preschool-age daughter, I'm constantly besieged with questions. While on an after-dinner walk, the enquiry comes up:

"Where's the sun gone?"

"He's sleeping."

"Why?"

"Because his mommy put him to bed."

"Why?"

"Because he has to go to preschool tomorrow."

"Why?"

"Because he likes playing with his friends and teachers."

"Why?"

A few more whys later, I'm ready to confess ignorance. Such a small question—Why?—yet so hard to answer. Fortunately, the "whats" are easier to tackle. As it happens, the English language has a word for almost everything around, from the disk on the top of a flagpole (truck), to the spot on a die or a domino (pip), to the little circle that comes out of a punched paper (we all know it by now—remember *chad*?). Let's take a look at some more words that answer, "What is this called?"

crossbuck (KROS-buk)
noun　An X-shaped warning sign at a highway-railroad crossing.
From *cross-* + *buck,* from *sawbuck.*

● Tony was prescient of the coming trend toward hyperspecial-
ization, and accordingly narrowed down his interest in railroad
memorabilia to collecting only *crossbucks* from various parts of
the world.

hallux (HAL-uhks), plural halluces (HAL-yuh-seez)
noun　Big toe. More generally, the innermost digit on the hind
foot of animals.
From Late Latin *hallux,* from Latin *hallus,* similar to *pollex* (thumb).
The hallux, by the way, is usually backward-directed in birds.

● Never one to lose a golden opportunity, Maria promptly filed
a product-liability suit against the furniture manufacturer after
she stubbed her *hallux* against the new side table in the middle
of the night.

septum (SEP-tuhm), plural septa (SEP-tuh)
noun　A dividing wall, in an animal or a plant. For example, the
partition between the nostrils.
From Latin *saeptum* (partition) from neuter of *saeptus,* past participle of *saepire* (enclose), from *saepes* (fence).

● Not able to decide whether to get her right nostril pierced or
her left one, Shania took the middle ground and went for the
septum.

● ● ●

I was court-martialed in my absence, and sentenced to death
in my absence, so I said they could shoot me in my absence.
—BRENDAN BEHAN, playwright (1923–1964)

ocellus (o-SEL-uhs), plural **ocelli** (o-SEL-eye)
noun 1. A small simple eye common to invertebrates. 2. An eye-like colored spot on an animal (as on peacock feathers, butterfly wings, fish, etc.) or on a leaf of a plant.
Latin *ocellus* (little eye), diminutive of *oculus* (eye).

● The newest fashion to come out of New York were *ocelli* patterns, and soon Liz's wardrobe was filled with dresses made with faux peacock feathers.

newel (NOO-el, NYOO-)
noun 1. A center column that supports the steps of a spiral staircase. 2. A post supporting the handrail of a staircase.
From Middle English *nowel,* from Middle French *nouel* (kernel), from Late Latin *nucalis* (nutlike), from Latin *nuc-, nux* (nut).

● As soon as he was crowned, the new king decided to put the billions lying in the state treasury to good use and ordered his assistant to encrust the royal palace—from *newel* to lintel—with jewels.

· · ·

The best cure for worry, depression, melancholy, brooding, is to go deliberately forth and try to lift with one's sympathy the gloom of somebody else.
—ARNOLD BENNETT, author (1867–1931)

CHAPTER 16

Words Formed by Metathesis

When you hear someone pronouncing *ask* as "aks" or pretty as "purty," do you find yourself looking down your nose? Not so fast! What you're witnessing is the English language busy at work, mutating, evolving, and refurbishing its word-stock, making things easier to pronounce. Known as metathesis, it is the same process that gave us *dirt* (from *drit*) and *curd* (from *crud!*). If you ever used the word *flimsy*, you did it: the word is the metathesized form of the word *filmsy*. It is somewhat like our friend *spoonerism* (see chapter 55), except that here the letters or sounds get transposed within the same word rather than between words. Many everyday words appear in a form created by such interchange of letters: the word *bird* came from Old English *brid, third* from *thridda*. Going back to *ask,* here is an interesting twist. The word *ask* itself came from two Old English forms *acsian* and *ascian* that coexisted. Eventually the latter won over and became standard. So what we are seeing here is history repeating itself. A few hundred years and who knows, we may be exhorting, "Aks not what your country can do for you."

scart (skart)

verb tr., intr.   To scratch, scrape, or scar.
Metathetic variation of *scrat* (to scratch).

● Halloween was a special time for Fitzgruff. During that time of the year, his listening choices changed from Mozart to the noise of cats *scarting* on the door and other assorted sounds.

prad (prad)

noun   Horse.
By metathesis from Dutch *paard* (horse).

● "Just send somebody out to relieve my mate, will you, young man?" said the officer; "he's in the gig, a-minding the *prad*. Have you got a coach 'us here, that you could put it up in, for five or ten minutes?"

—*Charles Dickens,* Oliver Twist *(1838)*

bort (bort)

noun   Poor-quality diamond, or diamond fragment, used as an industrial abrasive, as in a grinding wheel.
Possibly metathetic variation of *brot,* from Old English *gebrot* (fragment).

● When Heldebald continued to insist on even cheaper diamonds to give to his wife on her seventy-fifth birthday, the jewelry-store salesman politely referred him to the nearest hardware store for *bort*.

● ● ●

After I'm dead I'd rather have people ask why I have no monument
than why I have one.
—CATO THE ELDER, statesman, soldier, and author (234–149 B.C.E.)

gride (gryd)

verb intr.   To scrape or graze against an object to make a grating sound.
verb tr.   To pierce or cut with a weapon.
noun   A grating sound.
Metathetic variation of *gird*.

● And still within a hair's breadth of his ear
  The crunch and *gride* of wheels rings sharp and clear.
      —*Wilfrid Wilson Gibson, "Wheels,"* Poems *(1917)*

scrimmage (SKRIM-ayg)

noun.   1. A rough struggle. 2. A practice game, often between two parts of the same team. 3. A tussle for the ball in games such as football, rugby, or soccer.
verb tr., intr.   To engage in a scrimmage.
Middle English metathetic variant of *skirmish*.

● The concert ground was a scene of *scrimmage* among adolescent boys over a candy wrapper that was supposed to have been discarded by Britney Spears.

· · ·

At a dinner party one should eat wisely but not too well,
and talk well but not too wisely.
—W. SOMERSET MAUGHAM, author and playwright (1874–1965)

CHAPTER 17

Words Not to Put on Your Résumé

Have you ever been unfortunate enough to have to consult books about résumé preparation? If so, you would know that these tomes advise you to include in your résumé action words that are supposed to make you appear a performer, a go-getter, a man or woman of action. So if you follow their wisdom, you don't simply write, "I took the trash out on the graveyard shift at my neighborhood Bumpy's" as your work experience. Instead, you embellish: "As nocturnal sanitation superintendent of the local branch of a multi-billion-dollar food business, I implemented refuse collection policies and increased customer satisfaction by 27.9 percent." There! Doesn't it look much better now?

While we can't counsel you on how to adorn your life history, we can give you a few words you may want to avoid to describe yourself on that most important sheet of paper in your working life. Even though these words have an impressive sound, the words you see on this page are not the ones you want on your résumé.

manqué (mahng-KAY)

adjective   Frustrated in fulfillment of one's ambitions.
From French, from past participle of *manquer* (to lack), from Italian *mancare,* from *manco* (lacking), from Latin *mancus* (maimed).

● "Dad, meet my boyfriend, Fudwell, a rock star *manqué*. He currently works at the Hard Rock Cafe as a waiter." The last three words of this introduction can be conveniently spoken in a softer voice or omitted altogether.

distrait (di-STRAY)

adjective   Inattentive or absentminded.
From Middle English, from Old French, from Latin *distractus,* past participle of *distrahere* (to distract).

● Useful in writing recommendation letters: "It's my sincerest pleasure to report that Tantella was unmatched in the whole office when it came to being *distrait.*"

recreant (REK-ree-uhnt)

adjective or *noun*   Unfaithful, disloyal, traitorous, cowardly.
From Old French *recreire* (to yield), from Latin *credere* (to believe).

● Always truthful, if a bit evasive, Valia's resume read, "In my last job at the advertising agency, my creative abilities went hand-in-hand with my *recreant* nature."

garrulous (GAR-uh-luhs, GAR-yuh-)

adjective   A distinguished word to describe a blabbermouth, one prone to rambling.
From Latin *garrulus,* from *garrire* (to chatter).

● ● ●

You can discover what your enemy fears most by observing
the means he uses to frighten you.
—ERIC HOFFER, philosopher and author (1902–1983)

● The announcer burbled into the microphone, "My friends, it is with great joy that I introduce our *garrulous* speaker Theodemer."

truculent (TRUK-yuh-luhnt)
adjective   Hostile.
From Latin *truculentus*, from *truc-*, *trux* (savage).

● Especially useful word for writing honest personals: "A highly *truculent* woman in search of a truthful, sensitive man . . ."

. . .
I have discovered that all human evil comes
from this, man's being unable to sit still in a room.
—BLAISE PASCAL, philosopher and mathematician (1623–1662)

CHAPTER 18

A Verbal Zoo

This group of words is somewhat like a zoo—a prison for animals—where living sentient beings are captured and locked inside small enclosures. Instead, here we have animals encased inside the words. Find out how many of these animals you can identify and liberate from this verbal zoo.

welkin (WEL-kin)
noun   The vault of heaven, firmament; the sky.
From Middle English *welken,* from Old English *wolcen* (cloud).

● Against the *welkin* volleys out his voice;
  Another and another answer him,
  Clapping their proud tails to the ground below,
  Shaking their scratch'd ears, bleeding as they go.
                              —*Bill Shakespeare,* Venus and Adonis

aphelion (uh-FEE-lee-uhn, uh-FEEL-yuhn)
noun   The point in the orbit of a heavenly body that is farthest from the sun. (*Perihelion* is where it is the closest.)
From New Latin *aphelium,* from Greek *apo-* (apart) + *helios* (sun).

● Although Tom had been at the perihelion with respect to the Hollywood star Rowlia Jouberts when they were a couple, his fate and her taste had now changed, and he was relegated to the *aphelion*.

endogamy (en-DOG-uh-mee)
noun 1. Marrying within a similar social group. 2. Pollination among flowers of the same plant.
From Greek *endo-* (within) + *-gamy* (marriage).

● Even though her dentist parents reluctantly accepted it, they were not very pleased when Geeta, their surgeon daughter, married a tambourine player, flouting the family tradition of *endogamy*.

vamoose (va-MOOS, vuh-)
verb intr.   To leave in a hurry.
From Spanish *vamos* (let's go), from Latin *vadere* (to go).

● He (Eddie Cortez, mayor of Pomona, California) was stopped by border patrol agents one day last summer in his town, more than 100 miles from the Mexican border, and ordered to produce documents to prove he was a legal resident.

He wasn't doing anything suspicious. He was just sitting in his truck, wearing jeans and looking like he might be a Latino, which apparently is all it takes to look suspicious in the minds of some people.

Fortunately, as Cortez tells the story, he had a badge in his pocket that identified him as Pomona's mayor. Embarrassed, the border agents apologized and *vamoosed*.
—*Clarence Page, "Illegal Immigrants Are an Easy Target,"*
St. Louis Post-Dispatch *(June 15, 1994)*

• • •

What other dungeon is so dark as one's own heart!
What jailer is as inexorable as one's self!
—NATHANIEL HAWTHORNE, author (1804–1864)

epigone (EP-i-goan), also **epigon** (EP-i-gon)
noun   A mediocre imitator or follower of an important person such as an artist or writer.

From French *epigone,* singular of *epigones,* from Greek *epigonoi* (child), sons of the seven heroes against Thebes, from plural of *epigonos,* born after : *epi-* (after) + *gonos,* from root of *gignesthai* (to be born).

The term *epigonoi* (the later generation) was applied to the sons of the seven champions against Thebes, a city in ancient Greece.

● Soon after the artist Filimer's new podism movement grew in popularity, countless *epigones* began offering classes in the art of painting with toes.

• • •

The best effect of fine persons is felt after we have left their presence.
—RALPH WALDO EMERSON, philosopher and writer (1803–1882)

CHAPTER 19

Words from Medicine

An ounce of prevention is worth a pound of cure, so the saying goes. But sometimes no amount of prevention helps, and we are forced to visit those trained in the healing arts. Like any profession, the world of medicine has its own jargon. If you have come down with a bad case of medical jargonitis, help is near. Here is our prescription: take the five words in this chapter and e-mail us next week.

sternutation (stur-nyuh-TAY-shuhn)
noun   The act of sneezing or a sneeze.
From Middle English *sternutacioun,* from Latin *sternutatio,* from *sternutatus,* past participle of *sternutare,* frequentative of *sternuere* (to sneeze).

● The butler sneezed in the hallway, and the governess didn't miss the opportunity to inculcate good manners in little Roderick, "Mr. Godegisel, when someone performs a *sternutation* in your presence, the proper response is to enunciate, 'Gesundheit!'"

nosocomial (nos-uh-KO-mee-uhl)
adjective   Originating or acquired in a hospital. Used to refer to infections.
From Late Latin *nosocomium* (hospital) from Late Greek *nosoko-meion* (one who tends the sick).

● Galindus had been in the hospital for flu treatment. Later when his doctor explained that they had detected a case of *nosocomial* infection of measles, he feebly thanked her for her quick-diagnosis, unaware that he had contracted it in the hospital.

antitussive (an-tee-TUS-iv, an-ti-)
adjective   With properties of suppressing coughing.
noun   A substance that is used to relieve coughing, such as codeine or licorice.
From Greek *anti-* (opposite) + Latin *tussis* (cough).

● The nurse at the clinic had a vague foreboding that they didn't want to sign up that man as a patient when he informed her on the phone, "I'd like to see a physician for my symptoms of tussis and get a prescription for an *antitussive* agent."

prophylaxis (pro-fuh-LAK-sis, prof-)
noun   Measures taken for prevention of disease. In dentistry, this word also refers to the cleaning of teeth.
From New Latin, from Greek *prophylaktikos* (guarding).

A cousin of this word, *prophylactic,* refers to a rubber sheath used to prevent conception. In this age of AIDS and its numerous predecessors, the word is doubly suitable for the said device.

• • •

Action is eloquence.
—WILLIAM SHAKESPEARE, playwright and poet (1564–1616)

● Even though not as attentive to his own hygiene, Odotheus had been dutifully washing and waxing his car every Saturday afternoon as a *prophylaxis* for rusting.

aperient (uh-PIR-ee-uhnt)

adjective   Laxative; causing evacuation of the bowels.

noun   A mild laxative. Also called *aperitive.*

From Latin *aperient,* stem of *aperiens* (opening), present participle of *aperire* (to open).

● Obadiah had had a fascination with *aperients* since his early days, and, perhaps appropriately, his schoolbook had him named as the one most likely to be a gastroenterologist.

● ● ●

Inside my empty bottle I was constructing a lighthouse
while all the others were making ships.
—CHARLES SIMIC, poet (1938–)

CHAPTER 20

Semordnilap

A popular motivational saying goes, "*Desserts* is *stressed* spelled backward." *Desserts* is an example of a reversible word, which when read from the right yields another word. For that matter, so is *stressed*. All of the words in this chapter exhibit this quality. Just like reversible clothing that changes pattern when worn inside out, reversible words result in other usable words. A special case of reversible words is palindromes, which spell the same when reversed. So palindromes are a subset of reversible words, which in turn are a subset of anagrams. Another name for reversible words is *semordnilap,* a self-referential word coined by reversing the word *palindromes.*

Some words coined in this manner have actually entered the dictionary. Here are two examples: *yob* (a rowdy youth), coined by reversing *boy,* and *mho* (former unit of conductance), coined by reversing *ohm,* the unit of electrical resistance.

Taking inspiration from the above *desserts/stressed* example, can you make a sentence or a pithy aphorism using some word and its semordnilap? Don your wordsmith hats. Here is a helpful hint: you can elicit semordnilapic quality in many words by forming their plural, past tense, and so forth. Also, semordnilaps are especially useful in creating longer palindromic words. Here is a simple example: "Devil Dennis sinned, lived." Can you come up with something more interesting?

avid (avid)
adjective   1. Enthusiastic. 2. Greedy. 3. Marked by keen interest and enthusiasm.
From Latin *avidus,* from *avere* (to desire).

● *Avid* singing does not a diva make.

ogre (O-guhr)
noun   1. A monster in legends and fairy tales who feeds on humans. 2. An extremely ugly or cruel person.
From French, probably ultimately from Latin *Orcus* (god of the underworld).

● "Ergo, the *ogre* will then run away fearing for his life," concluded Cethegus, the hero of a preteen adventure series, as he calculated his next move in the latest novel.

debut (day-BYOO, DAY-byoo)
noun   A first public appearance of a person or a thing.
verb tr. and intr.   To appear or perform something for the first time.
adjective   Pertaining to the first appearance.
From French *début,* from *débuter* (to make the first stroke in a game), from *de-* + *buter,* from *but* (goal).

● Perhaps as an omen of her acting career, the *debut* of the actress playing Juliet ended with her tubed hair unraveling and getting caught in the props on the stage.

● ● ●

History is fables agreed upon.
—VOLTAIRE, philosopher (1694–1778)

nonet (no-NET)

noun   1. A combination of nine instruments or voices. 2. A composition written for such a combination.

From Italian *nonetto,* from diminutive of *nono* (ninth), from Latin *nonus.*

● The carpenter shop *nonet* relished singing whimsical musical tributes to pieces of woodwork such as tenon and mortise.

rebus (REE-buhs)

noun   Representation of words by using objects or symbols, often in the form of a puzzle.

From Latin *rebus* (ablative plural of *res*), from the phrase *non verbis sed rebus* (not by words but by things).

● The answer to the *rebus* showing a suber that represented a place was "Cork, Ireland."

• • •

Millions long for immortality who do not know what to do
with themselves on a rainy Sunday afternoon.
—SUSAN ERTZ, author (1894–1985)

CHAPTER 21

Words with Color as Metaphor

E ver wonder how our vocabulary is colored by the many hues of a rainbow? Often we use colors as symbols for ideas, thoughts, and concepts but do it with little logic. Take the color blue, for example. A *blue chip* stock is good to hold in one's portfolio, while we're chary of *blue-sky* stock. A *blue collar* worker is a manual laborer, yet a *bluestocking* is a woman with intellectual inclinations. A *bluenose* is a prude, but a *blue blood* is aristocratic. Even a computer would go crazy trying to make sense of this. No wonder we made artificial languages to program computers. Let's take a look at other words and phrases tinged with colors.

blue rinse (BLOO rins)
adjective   Of, related to, or made up of elderly women.
From the hair–dye used on gray hair that produces a blue shade.

● When his online chat partner disclosed that she was a student, Godiscus thought he was chatting with a nubile college girl, unaware that it was his *blue-rinse* neighbor taking continuing education classes in the local community college.

greenmail (GREEN-mayl)
noun   The practice of buying a large quantity of a company's stock as a hostile takeover measure, and then selling it back to the company at a higher price.
From *green* (money) + *mail* (as in blackmail).

● Hermangild had been a lawyer for a tobacco multinational for too long and opted to put his energies something relatively nobler. Now he was making a fortune *greenmailing* companies on Wall Street.

brown study (broun STUD-ee)
noun   A state of deep absorption in thought.
Apparently from *brown* in the sense of *gloomy*.

● The new shoe catalog had just come in mail and Imelda was lost in a *brown study*.

purple passage (PUR-puhl PAS-ij), also **purple patch, purple prose**
noun   1. A brilliant passage in an otherwise dull and uninspiring work. 2. A piece of writing marked by an ornate, florid style.
From Latin *pannus purpureus* (purple patch), a phrase used by poet Horace in his *Ars Poetica* (The Art of Poetry) to suggest a patch of royal fabric on an ordinary cloth.

● Gaiseric had high hopes for his 95,000-word epic detailing his protagonist's adventures in pig farming, but when the only good part in the review read, "does have a few *purple passages*," he decided he should keep his day job.

● ● ●

Iron rusts from disuse, stagnant water loses its purity, and in cold weather becomes frozen, even so does inaction sap the vigor of the mind.
—LEONARDO DA VINCI, painter, engineer, and scientist (1452–1519)

pink collar (PINGK KOL-uhr)

adjective   Pertaining to the type of jobs, such as telephone opera-
tor or secretary, traditionally held by women.

From the color pink, traditionally associated with women, on the
model of phrases *white collar* or *blue collar.*

● Ever on the alert for social shifts among the power elite, the
New York Times pointed out the other day that this is the year
in which women entering law school may, for the first time,
outnumber men. The *Times* drafted a number of learned ob-
servers to speculate on the meaning of it all: Perhaps the at-
mosphere of law schools will become more "teamlike."

...But the most interesting comment in the article came
from one Deborah Rhode, a Stanford law school professor who
worries that the law may become a *"pink collar* ghetto," like
other professions that have traditionally welcomed women.

—*Marjorie Williams, "Woman's Place Is at the Bar,"*
Washington Post *(April 4, 2001)*

● ● ●

Luck never gives; it only lends.
—SWEDISH PROVERB

CHAPTER 22

Words That Make One Say, "I Didn't Know There Was a Word for That!"

One doesn't have to know the unit of pain (dol) to realize that the unit of joy is not the dollar, or any other currency for that matter. We don't have to look far to discover that some of the richest people on this planet are not the happiest ones. Having lived in two not only geographic but also economically antipodal places, I've met people who were blissful and people who were miserable, but their conditions were hardly a function of money. Certainly it is good to have the means to pay for basic necessities, but after that it's only a series of zeros in a bank account.

English author Samuel Butler once said, "Words are like money; there is nothing so useless, unless when in actual use." We can't do much about circulating money (which we hope you have plenty of), but we do try our best to put words in actual use. Here are a few words that make one say, "I didn't know there was a word for that!"

dol (dol)

noun   A unit for measuring the pain intensity.
From Latin *dolor* (pain).

● I put my right hand in the hold and found the pipe that fed the radiator—God, it was hot. I took the pipe in thumb and forefinger, overriding the reflex to pull away. Two *dols,* three dols, five dols, yes, seven dols—maybe even eight dols. Eight dols and holding. Still eight. Wait. Seven and a half? Six and holding. Five dols, four dols. Four dols and steady.

Minutes later it was still a comfortable four dol—what did they do, shut off the steam? Finally I removed my hand and examined my fingers: great blisters on thumb and finger.

—*Richard Kopperdahl, on his adventures with this thing called life, in* "*Bettervue hospital,*" Village Voice *(October 3, 1995)*

murdrum (MUR-drum)

noun   1. The killing of someone in a secret manner. 2. The fine paid to the king by the village where such a crime occurred unless the killer was found.
From Medieval Latin, from Old French, *murdre* (murder).

This archaic word is one of many that had their origin in Old English law. If the perpetrator of a murder couldn't be found, the whole village (known as the *hundred*) had to pay the fine to the royalty, unless the victim was an Englishman (or woman). As you can guess, after the Norman Conquest such laws flourished. But what makes this word more interesting is that it is a palindrome (see chapter 20).

● A stuffed-toy collector had been killed in the middle of the night. Detective Theodahad had a number of leads in the *mur-*

• • •

I'm a great believer in luck and I find the harder I work, the more I have of it.
—THOMAS JEFFERSON, third U.S. president, architect, and author (1743–1826)

drum case, but the most promising seemed to be one where the motive was the theft of Beanie Babies.

thalweg (TAHL-veg, -vek)
noun   A line connecting the lowest point along the riverbed or in a valley.
From German *thal* (valley) + *weg* (way).

This line also serves as the boundary line between two states separated by a river.

● The two states had been constantly fighting over the use of river water and finally they chose to erect a dividing wall along the *thalweg*.

scurf (skurf)
noun   Scales or flakes, such as dandruff.
From Middle English, from Old English, from Old Norse *skurfa* (crust).

● The date between Luisa and Burleigh was going pretty well. They were leaning closer to each other on the dining table. If only he had thought of washing off his *scurfs* beforehand.

mora (MOR-uh)
noun   The unit of time equivalent to the ordinary or normal short sound or syllable.
From Latin *mora* (delay), hence, space of time.

● The writing instructor generally encouraged her students, but when she saw Euphemia's verse, her comment was terse: "One *mora* too many."

• • •

No really great man ever thought himself so.
—WILLIAM HAZLITT, essayist (1778–1830)

CHAPTER 23

Wordpix I

It's said that a picture is worth a thousand words. What if a word itself is a picture? That's the idea behind what I call wordpix—words presented so that they do their own show-and-tell. With each word in this chapter we'll feature its wordpix as well. Without further ado, let's see some words and let them talk about themselves.

verboten (vuhr–BOHT–n)
adjective   Not allowed; forbidden.
From German, past participle of *verbieten,* to forbid.

- "Verbing of nouns is *verboten,*" the high-school grammar teacher admonished.

VERB⊘TEN

supernumerary (soo–puhr–NOO–muh–rer–ee, –NYOO–)
adjective.   More than required; extra.
noun   1. A supernumerary person. 2. An actor who appears in a drama or film with no speaking part.

Latin *supernumerarius* (super, above-) + *numerus* (number).

In anatomy, the word *supernumerary* is used to refer to an extra tooth, a sixth finger, a third breast, and so forth (though in the case of the latter, the term *supermammary* might be more apt). Often a jury includes a supernumerary juror in case a juror drops out in the middle of a trial. In the army, a supernumerary guard is posted, just in case he is needed.

● When his boss wrote the word *supernumerary* in his performance review, Crousherd was ecstatic. Only when he got the pink slip next day did he realize he wasn't a super employee but a superfluous one.

SUPERNUMERARY¥

epicene (EP-i-seen)
adjective   Having characteristics of both sexes. 2. Effeminate.
noun   A person or object that is epicene.
From Middle English, from Latin *epicoenus,* from Greek *epikoinos,* *epi-* + *koinos* (common).

● This time I've bought a sweater that is *epicene* so either of us can wear it!" Mrs. Frugal chirped as she showed her husband the bright pink garment.

. . .
If I had eight hours to chop down a tree,
I'd spend six sharpening my axe.
—ABRAHAM LINCOLN, sixteenth U.S. president (1809–1865)

diastema (die-uh-STEE-mah), plural **diastemata**
(die-uh-STEE-muh-tuh)
noun   A gap between two adjacent teeth.
From Late Latin, from Greek *diastema* (interval), from *diastanai* (to put apart).

● The rock band Space Girls has made *diastemata* cool—no wonder teenage girls are flocking to dentists to have their teeth spaced.

DIASTE*W*A

ullage (UL-ij)
noun   The amount of liquid by which a container falls short of being full.
From Middle English *ulage,* from Old French *eullage,* from *eullier* (to fill a cask), from *ouil* (eye, hole), from Latin *oculus* (eye).

● "Is the gas tank half-empty or half-full?" Grouler wondered. He continued driving while pondering the *ullage,* and soon he was out of gas forty-seven miles from the nearest gas station.

ULLAGE

. . .

The supreme happiness in life is the conviction that we are loved.
—VICTOR HUGO, poet, author, and playwright (1802–1885)

CHAPTER 24

Wordpix II

chevron (SHEV-ruhn)
noun   A pattern or object in the shape of a *V* or an inverted *V.*
From Middle English, from Old French *chevron* (rafter), from Vulgar Latin *caprion* (stem of *caprio*), from Latin *caper* (goat.)

● To increase employee morale, the company president decided
   to award a cheap plastic *chevron* to those putting in more than
   seventy hours per week.

CHE⌄RON

maverick (MAV-uhr-ik)
noun   1. A person independent in thought and action. 2. An unbranded animal.
After Samuel A. Maverick (1803–1870), a cattle owner who left
his calves unbranded.

- Always a *maverick,* Annelet decided to get a Ph.D. on earthworms mating behavior instead of following her siblings to law school.

MAVERIC𝒦

pecuniary (pi-KYOO-nee-er-ee)
adjective   1. Relating to money. 2. Involving a monetary fine.
From Latin *pecuniarius,* from *pecunia* (property, wealth), derivative of *pecus* (cattle).

- When asked why he held up the bank, the robber replied, "Because that's where *pecuniary* objects are."

PECUNIARY

pariah (puh-RI-uh)
noun   An outcast.
From Tamil *paraiyar,* plural of *paraiyan* (drummer), people considered lower in rank in the former caste system of India.

- Sending spam or unsolicited e-mail is the fastest way to become a *pariah* on the Internet.

PARIA   H

· · ·

Until lions have their historians, tales of the hunt
shall always glorify the hunter.
—AFRICAN PROVERB

CHAPTER 25

Wordpix III

pendulous (PEN-juh-luhs, PEN-dyuh-, -duh-)
adjective   1. Hanging. 2. Undecided.
From Latin *pendulus,* from *pendere* (to hang).

● Charmed by his literary insights yet repelled by his slobbery eating habits, she remained *pendulous* about Fredfud's proposal.

PENDUL|US
O

acclivity (a-KLIV-i-tee)
noun   An upward slope.
From Latin *acclivitas,* from *acclivis* (uphill), from *ad-* + *clivus* (slope).
The opposite of this word is *declivity,* meaning "a downward slope."

● A few days on the neighborhood *acclivities,* and Fenton dropped his life goal of scaling Mt. Everest in favor of improving his bowling scores.

ACCLIVITY

kowtow (kow-TOW)
verb   To kneel and touch the forehead to the ground as a mark of
respect; to show servile deference.
noun   An act of kowtowing.
From Chinese *kou* (knock) + *tou* (head).

● When the head of the giant software corporation refused to
kowtow to the swami, he was promptly transformed into a little
bug.

KOWⱢOW

oology (oh-OL-uh-jee)
noun   The study of birds' eggs.
From Greek *o-* (egg) + *logy* (study).

● Oeufelia is a keen student of *oology.* Her idea of a perfect date
involves cataloguing eggs after watching a *National Geographic*
video.

OOLOGY

. . .

As against having beautiful workshops, studios, etc.,
one writes best in a cellar on a rainy day.
—VAN WYCK BROOKS, author and critic (1886–1963)

inebriety (in-i-BRY-i-tee)
noun   Drunkenness.
Intensive prefix *in-* + Latin *ebriare* (to make drunk), from *ebrius* (drunk).

● On receiving his third warning for *inebriety* while at work, Dipsom sent his resignation with the note, "This job interferes with my drinking."

INEBRIETY

CHAPTER 26

Words with Offbeat Pluralizations

So what is the plural form for the word *atlas? Atlases?* Yes, but not always. When used to refer to collections of maps, it is *atlases.* In architecture, however, where *atlas* is a standing or kneeling figure used as a column, the plural form of the word is *atlantes.* While the rules for pluralization in the English language are relatively simple, things do become muddled with exceptions, especially when the rules are inherited from the language the word came from. Let's take a look at words that pluralize in rather unusual ways.

opus (OH-pus), plural **opera** (OH-puhr-a, OP-uhr-a) or **opuses**

noun A musical or literary composition.
From Latin *opus* (work).

So what do we call a minor novel or a symphony? The diminutive form of *opus* is *opuscule.* And a great work is a *magnum opus.* But let's remember, an *octopus* is not a collection of eight *opera.*

● When she lost her *opus* to the latest virus that clobbered her disk containing her Great American Novel, only then did Gundela realize the importance of making proper backup.

occiput (OK-suh-put), plural occipita (ok-SIP-i-tah) or occiputs

noun   The back part of the head or skull.
From Middle English, from Latin *occipit*, from *oc-*, from *ob-* (against) + *ciput*, from *caput* (head).

Here are the opening lines of Ogden Nash's 1931 poem titled "Invocation," an ode to smut-busting Senator Reed Smoot of Utah:

● Senator Smoot (Republican, Ut.)
Is planning a ban on smut.
Oh root-ti-toot for Smoot of Ut.
And his reverent *occiput.*
Smite, Smoot, smite for Ut.
Grit your molars and do your dut.

chrysalis (KRIS-uh-lis), plural chrysalises (KRIS-uh-lis-es) or chrysalides (kri-SAL-i-deez)

noun   A pupa of a moth or butterfly, enclosed in a cocoon.
From Latin *chrysallis,* from Greek.
This word goes around spelled as *chrysalid,* too.

● Even at the ripe age of thirty-seven Roderic was living with his parents despite their numerous attempts to push him out of his *chrysalis.*

· · ·

Be slow in choosing a friend, slower in changing.
—BENJAMIN FRANKLIN, statesman, author, and inventor (1706–1790)

numen (NOO-muhn, NYOO-), plural **numina** (-muh-nuh)
noun   Divine power, deity, or spirit presiding in a place. Also, creative energy.
From Latin *numen* (nod, divine power).

● When Fernando's sculptures came up crooked one after another, he realized his *numen* was not happy.

virtuoso (vur-choo-OH-soh, -zos), plural **virtuosos** or **virtuosi**
(-see)
noun   1. Someone who has a special talent in a field, especially in music. 2. One with deep appreciation for something.
adjective   Of or pertaining to a virtuoso.
From Italian *virtuoso* (skilled), from Late Latin *virtuosus* (virtuous), from Latin *virtus.*

● Little Tommy loved to bang on his toy keyboard, much to the delight of his parents who saw a budding *virtuoso* in him.

● ● ●

Mistakes live in the neighbourhood of truth and therefore delude us.
—RABINDRANATH TAGORE, poet, philosopher,
and Nobel laureate (1861–1941)

CHAPTER 27

Words about Relations

While English has one of the most expansive vocabularies among languages, one area where it is easy to notice its impoverishment is in words to describe relations. When you introduce a bright young fellow as your brother-in-law, you don't really tell much. He could be any of the maybe half-dozen people in your kinship. On the other hand, many languages have words to describe even the most complicated relation concisely and unambiguously. In the Hindi language, for example, there are distinct words to spell out all possibilities of brothers-in-law, and in some cases, there are separate words that describe whether the bro-in-law is younger or older than the person through whom this relationship takes place. Let's enrich our verbal clan with some words about relations.

agnate (AG-nayt)
adjective   Related through the father's side or male side only.
noun   A relative whose relation is traceable through males only.
From Latin *agnatus,* past participle of *agnasci* (to become an agnate): *ad-* (in addition to) + *nasci* (to be born).

● When the octogenarian oil magnate kicked the bucket, his sole grandson suddenly found himself surrounded by dozens of people claiming to be his *agnates*.

miscegenation (mi-sej-uh-NAY-shuhn, mis-i-juh-)
noun   Marriage or cohabitation of a couple from different races. From Latin *miscere* (to mix) + *genus* (race) + *-ation*.

● In 1958, a Virginia interracial couple was found guilty of felony on account of *miscegenation*. The ironically named *Loving v. Virginia* went up to the Supreme Court and in 1967 ended in victory for Richard and Mildred Loving overturning their conviction and the punishment of a twenty-five-year exile. The dark ages weren't that far off, were they?

progenitor (pro-JEN-i-tuhr)
noun   1. A direct ancestor; forefather. 2. A precursor, originator, or founder.
From Middle English *progenitour*, from Old French *progeniteur*, from Latin *progenitor*, from *progenitus*, past participle of *progignere* (to beget), from *pro-* (forward) + *gignere* (to beget).

● Have we not lost most part of all the towns,
  By treason, falsehood and by treachery,
  Our great *progenitors* had conquered?
          —*Bill Shakespeare,* King Henry VI, Part I, *Act V, Scene IV*

enate (i-NAYT, EE-nayt), also **enatic**
adjective   Related on the mother's side.
noun   A person related on the mother's side.

· · ·

Talent develops in tranquillity, character in the full current of human life.
          —JOHANN WOLFGANG VON GOETHE, poet, author,
          and philosopher (1749–1832)

From Latin *enatus,* past participle of *enasci* (to issue out).

Enate is the female counterpart of the first word in this chapter: *agnate.* There is also another *-nate: cognate,* a handy unisex term for either *enate* or *agnate.* A *cognate* is one who shares the same ancestry. The term *cognate* is also used to refer to words that have descended from a common root either in the same or different languages. The words *regal* and *royal,* both derived from Latin *regalis,* are cognates. When the two cognates are from a single language, they are called *doublets.*

Then there are *false cognates,* also known as *false friends.* For example, the English words *duel* and *duo* have no connection, even though they appear to be related.

● Cousins Elda and Imel had a certain fondness for footwear that could only be explained by the fact that they were *enates,* tracing their lineage to a certain presidential spouse in recent world history.

primogenitor (pry-moe-JEN-i-tuhr)

noun The earliest ancestor. Also used to refer to an ancestor or a forefather.

From Late Latin *primogenitor,* from Latin *primo* (first) + *genitor* (begetter).

● It was not entirely proven, but that didn't stop Whitfield from claiming Abraham Lincoln as his *primogenitor* in his résumé. If only he had known that it was Abe who said, "I don't know who my grandfather was; I'm much more concerned to know what his grandson will be."

• • •

The best index to a person's character is how he treats people who can't do him any good, and how he treats people who can't fight back.
—ABIGAIL VAN BUREN, advice columnist (1918–)

CHAPTER 28

Collective Nouns

The English language is rich in words that describe groups and collections, whether things, places, or living beings; a bouquet of roses, a flight of stairs, a cast of actors, and so on. What is even more fascinating are words—often poetic, and occasionally descriptive—used to denote groups of animals, such as a school of fish, a pride of lions, or a murder of crows.

Here are a few lesser-known terms used for collections of specimens from the animal kingdom. There are proper terms for almost all animals, but one can't just say "a bunch of this" or "a bunch of that." In fact, some animals take different group nouns depending on where they happen to be. A group of ducks are "a paddling" only if in water; in flight they become "a team."

Next time you camp out in the wilds and receive a visit from some uninvited guests in the form of, say, boars, you'll know what to say: "Help, I'm surrounded by a sounder of swine!" Anything else and the ranger may not come to your rescue. How about coining some new words for collections? A diction of word junkies? A linkup of webmasters? A bugaboo of computer programs? Can you think of some creative group nouns?

sounder (SOUN-duhr)

noun   1. A person or thing that makes sound. 2. A group of wild boars.

From Old French *sundre.*

 Suerid's friends have had a bit too much beer at his bachelor party and now they could best be described as a *sounder* of swine.

nide (nyde)

noun   A nest or a group of pheasants.

From Latin *nidus* (nest).

 On the first day of Christmas,
My true love gave to me:
A *nide* of pheasants...

skein (skayn)

noun   1. A length of yarn wound around a reel. 2. A flock of geese, ducks, or other similar birds in flight. 3. Something suggesting complex twists and tangles.

From Middle English *skeyine,* from Old French *escaigne.*

When in flight, geese are a *skein;* when not in flight, they are a *gaggle;* and when flying in a V formation, they are referred to as a *wedge.*

 Uncle Phedrus's tales of duck-hunting involved *skeins* in more than one sense of the word.

* * *

The unluckiest insolvent in the world is the man whose expenditure of speech is too great for his income of ideas.
—CHRISTOPHER MORLEY, author (1890–1957)

Here is a bunch of collective nouns from the world of computers and the Internet:

An *array* of programmers

A *clique* of computer mice

A *sneer* of Mac users

An *obfuscation* of user manuals

A *404* of former web sites

A *cylinder* of CDs

A *wildcard* of hackers

A *hindrance* of tech-support people

A *blizzard* of AOL disks

skulk (skulk)

verb intr.   To hide, evade, or move stealthily.

noun   1. Someone who lies in hiding, evades, or lurks. 2. A pack of foxes.

From Middle English *skulken,* of Scandinavian origin.

● Rock star Samantha Fuchs had come up with the perfect device—a burga—to allow her to *skulk* and keep her fans from chasing her.

• • •

Every man is a damned fool for at least five minutes every day.
Wisdom consists in not exceeding the limit.
—ELBERT HUBBARD, author, editor, and printer (1856–1915)

Pals

A few years ago, Margaret Thatcher invited some ex–prime ministers for a get-together at 10 Downing Street. I think it was Harold Macmillan, Harold Wilson, and James Callaghan. While they were there, Thatcher speculated about the proper word denoting a group of prime ministers. Macmillan suggested that the correct term would be *a lack of principals.*

—*Lydia Rivlin, London, United Kingdom*

bevy (BEV-ee)

noun   1. A group of birds or animals, especially larks, quail, or roe buck. 2. A group or collection.

From Middle English *bevey.*

In the United Kingdom, *bevy* is also an abbreviation for beverage.

● Savvy Al loved to chase a *bevy* of curvies in his Chevy.

• • •

A friend is a person with whom I may be sincere.
Before him I may think aloud.
—RALPH WALDO EMERSON, philosopher and author (1803–1882)

CHAPTER 29

Positive Words

Why do we have so much negativity around us? Open a newspaper, watch TV, listen to the radio, and you find nothing but negative words. Ever wonder why some words almost always appear in their negative forms? Here are some words that are completely scrutable, and a quick peek in the dictionary shows that these are licit formations. Use these words in your writing for a gainly touch, a couth appearance. We hope you feel gruntled with these words.

sipid (SIP-id)
adjective Savory; having a pleasing taste.
Back formation from *insipid*.

● Soon after Erwig took over the helm of the ailing television channel, he replaced its *sipid* programming with mud-wrestling and other features of that ilk, and the network swept the ratings.

pervious (PUR-vee-uhs)
adjective 1. Permeable; open to passage or penetration. 2. Open to suggestions, arguments, reason, change, and so forth.
From Latin *pervius,* from *per-* (through) + *via* (way).

● In the end, the company CEO proved *pervious* to reason and dropped his pet project of manufacturing pure drinking water for sale in superstores.

vincible (VIN-suh-buhl)

adjective   Defeatable; capable of being overcome.

From Latin *vincibilis,* from *vincere* (to overcome).

● "They had a lead of 21–0 and still the Eagles, who were both *pervious* and *vincible,* beat them, 35–30."

> —*Steve Jacobson, making ept use of the two words,*
> *in* Newsday *(October 4, 1993)*

furl (furl)

verb tr.   To roll up something, such as a flag.

verb intr.   To become rolled up.

noun   The act of rolling up or something rolled up.

From French *ferler,* from Old French *ferlier* (to fasten), from *fer, ferm* (firm) + *lier* (to tie), from Latin *ligare.*

● The annual conference of the National Quiltmakers Association ended with thousands of participants *furling* their handiwork.

requite (ri-KWYT)

verb tr.   To repay, return for, avenge, or retaliate.

From Middle English *re-* + obsolete *quiten* (to pay), a variant of *quit.*

● The utopian novelist's book chronicled a world in which everyone flossed after dinner, all Internet connections were high-speed, and where love was always *requited.*

• • •

True friendship is a plant of slow growth, and must undergo and withstand the shocks of adversity before it is entitled to the appellation.
—GEORGE WASHINGTON, first U.S. president (1732–1799)

CHAPTER 30

Discover the Theme II

The Rorschach test, named after Swiss psychiatrist Hermann Rorschach (1884–1922), aims to discover the personality of a person when it can't be found by the usual questions. The subject is shown random inkblot designs and asked to interpret them. The same inkblot may appear as clouds to one person, an elephant to another, or the face of a woman to a third.

Well, this collection of five words may seem quite like this test, but it isn't. The words here may appear to be selected with no design, but they do have a common theme. There is a definite property that a word has to fulfill before making an appearance here. And your mission, should you choose to accept it, is to identify that common trait. The answer is on page 193.

dekko (DEK-oh)
noun   A look.
From Hindi *dekho* (look), imperative of *dekhna* (to look).

● Little Achilles had cut the cake, and now he wished his birthday party would end soon so that he could take a *dekko* at the gifts.

ait (ayt), also, **eyot**
noun   A small island, especially one in a river.
From Middle English *eit,* from Old English diminutive of *ig* or *ieg* (island).

● Fog everywhere. Fog up the river, where it flows among green *aits* and meadows; fog down the river, where it rolls defiled among the tiers of shipping and the waterside pollutions of a great (and dirty) city.
                              —*Charles Dickens,* Bleak House *(1853)*

Eight Mates Date

The first time I heard the word *ait* was also the occasion of my first excursion to Cambridge, England. My date, I, and three other couples had lunch at a pub called the Fort St. George. The FSG is on a (former) island on the Cambridge River. The island was joined to the mainland centuries ago during one campaign or another, when the king's forces poured tons of dirt into the river.

We ran into friends several hours later who asked about our day. My friend Susan replied, "We eight ate on the ait."
                              —*Barbara Jungbauer, St. Paul, Minnesota*

---

bijou (BEE-zhoo, bee-ZHOO), plural **bijoux** (-zhoo, -zhooz)
noun   A small, delicate jewel or ornamental object of delicate workmanship.
From French, from Breton *bizou* (jeweled ring), from *biz* (finger).

● And then the revelation hit him. Those *bijou* handbags were not made to be carrying things. They were things in themselves.

• • •

The wastebasket is a writer's best friend.
—ISAAC BASHEVIS SINGER, author and Nobel laureate (1904–1991)

horst (horst)

noun A part of the earth's crust, surrounded by faults, that has risen upwards.

From German *horst* (thicket).

Graben is the counterpart of *horst*—the portion of crust that is surrounded by faults and has descended.

● Aldornia, the geologist, had a penchant for making unusual discoveries, so she was quite pleased when she found a *horst* of a different color during one of her expeditions.

dotty (DOT-ee)

adjective Eccentric, mentally unbalanced, unconventional.

From Scots *dottle* (fool), from Middle English *doten* (to dote).

● How time changes things! Paying people to surf the web ... what was considered a great inspiration in the dot-com boom becomes clearly a *dotty* little scheme during the dot-com bust.

● ● ●

A pedestal is as much a prison as any small space.
—GLORIA STEINEM, women's rights activist and editor (1934–)

CHAPTER 31

Lesser-Known Synonyms of Everyday Words

We all believe the first to scale Mt. Everest were Edmund Hillary and Tenzing Norgay, but the answer may be different. In 1924, a bold mountain climber, George Herbert Leigh Mallory, along with Andrew Irvine, attempted to reach the top of Mt. Everest. They were last sighted near the summit by the expedition's geologist, 2,000 feet below them. In 1999, Mallory's body—still intact after 75 years—was discovered by a group of climbers. Were Mallory and Irvine on their way up or coming down? We don't know, and perhaps never will, unless other climbers find Irvine's body and his camera that may yield clues. Mallory's grandson George Mallory II reached the summit in 1995.

When asked why one should climb a mountain, Mallory's famous answer was, "Because it's there." The words collected in this chapter should perhaps be used in the same spirit. Why use these words when other similar words exist? Just because they're there in the dictionary. Here are some words that are less well-known synonyms of everyday words.

athenaeum (ath–uh–NEE–um), also **atheneum**
(ath–uh–NEE–um)

noun   1. A library or reading room. 2. A literary or scientific club.
From Latin *Athenaeum,* from Greek *Athenaion* (a temple of
Athena, the goddess of wisdom).

Athenaeum is also used in Europe for a certain type or level of
high school. In Columbus, Ohio, there is a bar called Library, conveniently located near the Ohio State University campus. This es-
tablishment's somewhat misleading name has allowed countless
students to say to their parents, in all honesty, "Hi, Mom, sorry I
missed your call last night. I was at the Library." The marketing
genius behind Library is now probably busy drawing blueprints
for a casino called *Athenaeum.*

● Clia, the bibliophage *[see chapter 54],* knew that the best place
to find like-minded men would be the *athenaeum.*

tokology (to–KOL–uh–jee), also **tocology**

noun   Midwifery or obstetrics.
From Greek *tokos* (child, childbirth) + *-logy.*

The Greek word *tokos,* meaning "child," is also the word for
interest on capital deposit. Isn't interest the "child" of the capital?
In India, a popular saying goes, "Interest is dearer than principal."
It works on several levels. To the moneylender, interest on money
lent is more precious. On the other hand, to the borrower, the interest turns out to be dearer—more expensive—than the principal, especially when the money is borrowed from a loan shark.
And the best interpretation of all is when a grandparent says this
when referring to the grandchild!

A *tokodynamometer,* or *tokometer,* is an instrument that measures
contractions in an expectant mother during labor.

● ● ●

No soul is desolate as long as there is a human being
for whom it can feel trust and reverence.
—GEORGE ELIOT (MARY ANN EVANS), author (1819–1880)

● When the expectant woman asked the *tokology* physician what the most reliable way to determine baby's sex was, the jocund doctor answered, "Childbirth."

debark (di-BARK)
verb tr., intr.   To disembark.
From French *debarquer, de-* (from) + *barque* (ship).

debark (dee-BARK)
verb tr.   To remove the bark from a log or a dog.
From *de-* + *bark.*

● And then, in her most twee voice, the flight attendant cooed over the public-address system, "Welcome to Flight 913. If you're traveling with a dog, please *debark* your canine friend till you reach your destination and have *debarked* from the plane."

sartorial (sar-TOR-ee-uhl)
adjective   Related to a tailor or tailored clothes.
From Late Latin *sartor* (tailor).
   The word *sartorial* word has a cousin, *sartorius,* a long narrow muscle in the leg and the longest muscle in humans. What would tailored clothes have in common with a muscle of the leg? *Sartorius* is so named because it is concerned with the cross-legged position of tailors at work.

● She wasn't that averse to Methusaleh, but she wished he were a bit more interested in the state of world affairs than in the *sartorial* choices of soap stars.

● ● ●

The belly is the reason why man does not mistake himself for a god.
—FRIEDRICH NIETZSCHE, philosopher (1844–1900)

cancrine (KANG-krin)

adjective   1. Reading the same backwards as forwards; palindromic. 2. Crablike.

From Latin *cancr-* (stem of *cancer*) + *-ine.*

Here is a cancrine text, one with a complete story in it: A man, a plan, a canal: Panama.

Here is another that works on the word level instead of the letter level as in the previous example: "So patient a doctor to doctor a patient so!"

Crabby Music

J. S. Bach's Crab Canon is an example of cancrine music. It can be read—and played—from start to finish or from finish to start. Put the music sheet upside down? No problem! You can still play it and it will sound the same. You can see this curious piece of music for yourself on the web. Just go to http://www.btinternet.com/~derek.hasted/takeaway/crab.html

• • •

To love is to admire with the heart; to admire is to love with the mind.
—THEOPHILE GAUTIER, author (1811–1872)

CHAPTER 32

Words from Speeches

The eloquence of words combined with the art of oratory has given birth to speeches that have changed the course of history. These are the words that have inspired men and women to excel, moved their hearts, led them to action, provided comfort in times of trouble, guided them, and influenced them by example. Here are a few words taken from some famous speeches from history.

Of course, when reading or listening to many modern-day speakers, we have to be careful not to pay too much attention to empty words, for words don't mean a thing unless accompanied by deeds that match them. With professional speechwriters in tow, it is easy to sing lofty words while acting otherwise.

manacle (MAN-uh-kul)
noun 1. A shackle for the hand; handcuff. 2. Restraints.
verb tr. 1. To handcuff; fetter. 2. To restrain.
From Middle English, *manicle,* from Middle French, from Latin, diminutive of *manus* (hand).

English uses the Latin word for *hand*—*manus*—to form the word *manacle,* but in Spanish the word for manacles is *esposas* (wives).

● Five score years ago, a great American, in whose symbolic shadow we stand, signed the Emancipation Proclamation.... One hundred years later, the life of the Negro is still sadly crippled by the *manacles* of segregation and the chains of discrimination. One hundred years later, the Negro lives on a lonely island of poverty in the midst of a vast ocean of material prosperity.

> —*Martin Luther King Jr., "I Have a Dream,"*
> *Washington, D.C. (August 28, 1963)*

chasm (KAZ-um)

noun   1. A deep hole; gorge. 2. A sudden interruption, discontinuity. 3. A difference of ideas, beliefs, or opinions.
From Latin *chasma,* from Greek *khasma.*

● Today all of us do, by our presence here, and by our celebrations in other parts of our country and the world, confer glory and hope to newborn liberty.... The time for the healing of the wounds has come. The moment to bridge the *chasm* that divides us has come.

> —*Nelson Mandela, "Let Freedom Reign,"*
> *Presidential Inaugural Address, Pretoria, South Africa (May 10, 1994)*

attainder (uh-TAYN-duhr)

noun   Loss of property and civil rights of a person outlawed or sentenced to death.
From Middle English, from Old French *ataindre,* to accuse.

● ● ●

Why is it that we rejoice at a birth and grieve at a funeral?
It is because we are not the person involved.
—MARK TWAIN, author and humorist (1835–1910)

● Friends and fellow-citizens! I stand before you tonight under
   indictment for the alleged crime of having voted at the last
   presidential election, without having a lawful right to vote....
   For any State to make sex a qualification that must ever result
   in the disfranchisement of one entire half of the people is to
   pass a bill of *attainder* or an ex post facto law, and is therefore a
   violation of the supreme law of the land.

   —*Susan B. Anthony, U.S. suffragist, "Are women persons?*
   Speaking in response to a verdict of guilty of the crime
   of voting while being a woman" (June 17, 1873)

sentient (SEN-shent)

adjective   1. Capable of perception by sense; conscious. 2. Sensitive
in perception.
noun   Someone or something that has sensation.
From Latin *sentient*, present participle of *sentire* (to feel).

● It doesn't matter what the other's attitude is, whether negative
   or positive. What matters is that it is a human being, a *sentient*
   being that has the experience of pain and pleasure.

   —*Dalai Lama, Nobel Peace Prize acceptance speech*
   (December 10, 1989)

mirabile dictu (mee-RAH-bi-lay DIK-too)

interjection   Strange to say; wonderful to relate.
The earliest example of this Latin term is found in Virgil's *Aeneid*.
It literally means "wonderful to relate."

· · ·

A good laugh and a long sleep are the best cures in the doctor's book.
—IRISH PROVERB

● A hot-air balloon drifts slowly over a bottomless chasm, carrying several passengers.... Back in the balloon, something
longed-for and heartening has happened. On this occasion,
mirabile dictu, the many have not been sacrificed but saved.

> —*Salman Rushdie, "What is my single life worth?" A speech on the oc-
> casion of the 200th Anniversary of the First Amendment, delivered at the
> Columbia Graduate School of Journalism, New York (December 1991)*

· · ·
Choose the life that is most useful,
and habit will make it the most agreeable.
—FRANCIS BACON, essayist, philosopher, and statesman (1561–1626)

CHAPTER 33

Words That Contain the Vowels AEIOU Once and Only Once

"I'd like to buy a vowel." Most of us in the "civilized" world are familiar with this oft-heard sentence from a popular TV game show. For those who are not, it is a Hangman-like game where contestants identify words in several categories by guessing their letters. Correctly guessing a consonant helps in winning a prize, while one has to pay to guess a vowel. Imagine playing this game and getting words having all five vowels! It wouldn't be very exciting to have to squander all your cash in buying the vowels. To make it more tolerable, we've selected words that have all the vowels once, but only once. And the vowels can be in any order. To see the words with all the vowels, once and only once, AND in order, look at the sidebar on the last page of this chapter.

armigerous (ahr-MIJ-ehr-us)

adjective   Bearing or entitled to bear heraldic arms.
From Latin *armi-* (arms) + *-ger* (bearing) + *ous.*

● Charles Remismund was in a state of bliss on discovering the enterprising company that sold dukeships, lordships, and the like through the Internet. Now he proudly displays the *armigerous* privileges he got in exchange for $195 and insists that everyone address him as Lord Remismund, instead of calling him Charlie.

epuration (ep-yuh-RAY-shun)

noun   Purification, especially removal of officials or politicians believed to be disloyal; purge.
From French *epuration, epurer* (to purify).

● The company president's profound dislike for Beanie Babies resulted in an *epuration,* and all those displaying the Beanies in their office were forced to resign one by one.

Housing Dissidence

The word *epuration* had me doing a double take! Living in Quebec, I sometimes absorb French words into my English thoughts without realizing it. *Centre d'epuration* is a common sign around here ... it signifies a water purification plant. Upon reading the English definition, however, with its "especially removal of officials or politicians believed to be disloyal," I had the sudden mental image of all those plants being secretly used to house political dissidents! It is always interesting to realize how our use of words affects our perception of things.

—*Gail Charette, Boisbriand, Quebec, Canada*

● ● ●

Poetry is made out of our quarrel with ourselves.
—WILLIAM BUTLER YEATS, poet, playwright, essayist,
and Nobel Prize winner (1865–1939)

inquorate (in-KWO-rayt)
adjective   A meeting attended by too few people to form a quorum (the minimum number of members required to be present for valid transaction of business).
From Latin *quorum,* literally "of whom," from the wording of the commission issued to designate members of a body.

● Morris had the faint suspicion his Society for Straightforward Spelling was going to be short-lived, as membership had slumped to a handful and meetings were often *inquorate.*

ossuary (OSH-oo-eh-ree), plural **ossuaries,** also, **ossuarium.**
noun   A place or container for depositing the bones of the dead.
From Late Latin *ossuarium,* from neuter of Latin, *ossuarius* (of bones), from Old Latin *ossua,* plural of *oss-, os* (bone).

● Some have skeletons in their closets, and then there was Athaulf, who could best be described as having a whole *ossuary.*

uvarovite (oo-VAR-uh-vyt, yoo-)
noun   An emerald-green mineral, a variety of garnet.
After Count Sergei Semenovich Uvarov (1785–1855), president of the St. Petersburg Academy.

● Erelieva liked to call herself down-to-earth as she had a special fondness for earthy—if only a little precious—things such as, diamonds, *uravovites,* and sapphires.

* * *

All a man can betray is his conscience.
—JOSEPH CONRAD, novelist and short-story writer (1857–1924)

Here are a few words with all the vowels once and only once, and in order. You can even add *-ly* at the end to include the sometime vowel *y*.

facetious: not serious; jocular

abstemious: sparing; moderate

aerious: airy

annelidous: like a worm

The shortest word with each vowel used once is the name of perhaps the largest tree: *sequoia*.

And words with all the vowels once and only once and in reverse order:

uncomplimentary: not flattering; derogatory

duoliteral: having only two letters, such as *aa*, the Hawaiin word for *lava*

subcontinental: pertaining to a subcontinent

. . .

Simplicity doesn't mean to live in misery and poverty. You have what you need, and you don't want to have what you don't need.
—CHARAN SINGH, mystic (1916–1990)

CHAPTER 34

Coined Words II

In a previous chapter we saw a number of coined words. The word *linguaphile* (one who loves words and languages), which I coined back in 1994, finally found a place in a dictionary six years later (in the *American Heritage Dictionary,* 4th ed.).

Chances are you, too, have coined a word at one time and wondered how it could be made more popular. And can it reach the ultimate destination to grace the pages of a dictionary? How do you win that honor for your little baby? It's not easy. Share it with family and friends, use it, and encourage them to publish letters, articles, and stories using that word. And even if it doesn't make it into the dictionary, remember that it is still a bona fide word—nothing in the definition of the word *word* says that a word has to be in a dictionary to be called one. Have fun coining words, and enjoy these coinages that *did* reach the dictionaries.

eustasy (YOO-stuh-see)
noun   A uniform global change in sea level.
From *eustatic,* from German *eustatisch,* coined by Austrian geologist Edward Suess (1831–1914).

● Homer's ecstasy on buying a beachfront bungalow was short-lived as he read about *eustasy* in the next morning's newspaper.

Pangaea (pan-JEE-uh), also **Pangea**

noun   A supercontinent that existed when all the major land-masses of the earth were joined.

From Greek *pan-* (all) + *gaia* (earth), supposedly coined by German meteorologist Alfred Wegener (1880–1930), who first proposed the theory of plate tectonics and continental drift.

● Livila was truly afraid of flying and longed for the good old days in *Pangaea,* when the earth's whole landmass was together and she could drive to anywhere in a car.

McJob (mehk-JOB)

noun   A low-paying, non-challenging job with few benefits or opportunities, typically in the service sector.

Coined by Douglas Coupland in his 1991 novel *Generation X,* after McDonald's fast-food chain.

● Perhaps Vandalarius had read too many stories of people starting in the mailroom and rising to the top of the company, since he had no doubt one day he would advance from his *McJob* of flipping burgers at Tanny's to being the company president.

locust years (LO-kuhst yeers)

noun   A period of economic hardship.

Coined by British prime minister Winston Churchill to refer to the mid-1930s in Britain, after "the years that the locust hath eaten" from the Bible (Joel 2:25).

● Ammius was at a loss to understand what was going around. Typically the years of war were considered *locust years,* and

● ● ●

The sole meaning of life is to serve humanity.
—LEO TOLSTOY, author (1828–1910)

here the leaders were exhorting people to spend, travel, enjoy, eat, drink, and be merry.

prehensile (pri-HEN-sil, -syl)
adjective   1. Capable of seizing or grasping, especially by wrapping around. 2. Skilled at keen perception or mental grasp of an idea or concept. 3. Greedy.
From French *prehensile,* coined by French naturalist Georges Louis Leclerc De Buffon (1707–1788), from Latin *prehensus.*

● *A child's* prehensile *hand wrapped around an adult's fingers—what could be a purer example of trust!*

• • •

The two most engaging powers of an author are
to make new things familiar, and familiar things new.
—SAMUEL JOHNSON, lexicographer (1709–1784)

CHAPTER 35

English as a Global Language

English is a global language. With the rise of electronic comunication, worldwide trade, and international travel, its status has far surpassed that of a link language. English is equated with success. Wherever you go—from the luxuriant rain forests of Costa Rica to the untamed wilds of the Serengeti to the hodge-podge of Eastern bazaars—you're sure to find someone who speaks English, albeit in an accent far different from yours. If nothing else, English makes a disguised appearance in hybrids such as Franglais, Spanglish, and Hinglish.

Of course, this rise in popularity of English is not without a downside. Talk with someone for whom English is not a first language and you sense a feeling of loss. Reactions vary greatly—from the trace of helplessness of parents whose children can't appreciate a poem in their native language, to lawmakers making it mandatory for a company to have a web site in the country's official language before it can do business there.

There are already thousands of newspapers around the world published in the English language. What do you think about the spread of English? Could English one day be the Esperanto of the world? While you ponder this, here are a few words taken from the world's newspapers.

nous (noos, nous)
noun   1. Mind, intellect. 2. Common sense.
From Greek *noos, nous* (mind).

● The downfall of tyrant Slobodan Milosevic in a relatively peaceful people's revolution has created hope and despair in equal measure among those whose political *nous* tells them that this triumph of the Serbian people could have a serious ripple effect right here in Harare and other major centres of political dissent.

> —*Diana Mitchell, "Bells of Belgrade toll for Zimbabwe,"*
> *in Zimbabwe's* Financial Gazette *(October 12, 2000)*

dyscalculia (dis-kal-KYOO-lee-uh)
noun   Difficulty in solving math problems.
From Greek combining form *dys-* (ill or bad) + *calcul*(ate) + *-ia*.
An extreme case of dyscalculia is *acalculia,* an inability to solve math problems at all.

● Almost seven out of a hundred pupils suffer from *dyscalculia*—a learning disability that diminishes their mathematical ability but does not affect their general intelligence.

> —*Judy Siegel-Itzkovich, about the dyslexia of numbers,*
> *in Israel's* Jerusalem Post *(October 15, 1995)*

● ● ●

In the mountains of truth you never climb in vain.
—FRIEDRICH NIETZSCHE, philosopher (1844–1900)

timorous (TIM-uhr-uhs)
adjective Full of fear, timid.
From Middle English, from Middle French *timoureus,* from Medieval Latin *timorosus,* from Latin *timor* (fear), from *timere* (to fear).

Robert Burns (1759–1796) put this word to delightful use in his 1785 poem "To a Mouse." Here are the opening lines:

> Wee, sleekit, cowrin, tim'rous beastie,
> O, what a panic's in thy breastie!

- For years the Punjab University, in thrall to a student mafia, has had more to do with politics and less with education. The only answer to its problems is to shut it down indefinitely, disband its tainted and *timorous* faculty (or post it out where it can do the least harm), and make a fresh start.
  —*Ayaz Amir, on the politicization of education,*
  in Pakistan's Dawn *(June 30, 2000)*

soporific (sop-uh-RIF-ik, so-puh-)
adjective 1. Causing sleep. 2. Drowsy.
noun Something that that induces sleep.
From Latin *sopor* (a deep sleep).

- Indeed, Kapil will be judged as much by his effect on the team as his ability to stir the *soporific* BCCI.
  —*Rohit Brijnath, about the Indian cricket team*
  and its managing body, in India Today *(October 4, 1999)*

• • •

Often you must turn your stylus to erase,
if you hope to write anything worth a second reading.
—HORACE, poet and satirist (65–8 B.C.E.)

morose (mo-ROS)
adjective   Gloomy, sullen.
From Latin *morosus* (peevish), equivalent to *mor-, mos* (will, inclination) + *-osus, -ose.*

● Celebrating, though, is hardly the right word for the *morose* Vitukhnovskaya, a peculiar mix of teenage anxieties and deconstructionalist ideas.
> —*Natalya Shulyakovskaya, "Freed Poet Reflects on Time in Jail,"*
> The Moscow Times *(May 14, 1998)*

• • •

I shut my eyes in order to see.
—PAUL GAUGUIN, painter (1848–1903)

CHAPTER 36

Eponyms

The idea of Fletcherizing (to chew food many times) invites the question, "Is too much of a good thing better?" Horace Fletcher proposed that one should grind food once for each tooth in the mouth. That implies that we masticate each bite of pizza as many as thirty-two times. I'd rather stick with the idea that each byte has eight bits. At any rate, Mr. Fletcher, the art dealer turned nutritionist, did earn the moniker "The Great Masticator," for his popular book at the time, and got his name into the dictionary. Here are a few more such words, known as eponyms, coined after people from fact and from fiction.

Fletcherize (FLECH-uh-ryz)
verb tr., intr.   To chew food thoroughly.
From the practice of chewing food many, many times as advocated by Horace Fletcher, U.S. nutritionist (1849–1919).

● Fred's constant goading to *Fletcherize* was beginning to take effect as the muffled sound of teeth grinding had quietly replaced the dinner table conversation.

grinch (grinch)
noun   Someone who ruins others' enjoyment.
From the Grinch, a character in *How the Grinch Stole Christmas* (1957), by Dr. Seuss, pseudonym of Theodor Seuss Geisel (1904–1991).

●   Argos was engrossed in the gripping novel and looking forward to the denouement, unaware that some *grinch* had torn off the last page of the book before returning it to the library.

John Bull (jon bul)
noun   1. A personification of England or the English people. 2. A typical Englishman.
After John Bull, a character in John Arbuthnot's satire, *Law Is a Bottomless Pit* (1712).

●   It may be a little hard to understand why the average American has such a fascination for *John Bull's* accent.

aristarch (AR-uh-stark)
noun   A severe critic.
After Aristarchus of Samothrace (circa 216–144 B.C.E.), Greek philologist and critic of the Homeric poetry, who rejected many lines of it as spurious.

●   Few knew it but behind that *aristarch* in the Sunday newspaper lay a writer manque (see chapter 17).

Chicken Little (CHIK-en LIT-l)
noun   A pessimist-cum-alarmist, one who constantly warns of the possibility of calamities.

● ● ●

All you need in this life is ignorance and confidence,
and then success is sure.
—MARK TWAIN, author and humorist (1835–1910)

After a hen in a children's tale who, when hit on the head by a falling acorn, believes the sky is falling.

● It's a bit disingenuous to call the researchers alerting us of global warming *Chicken Littles* when we know many island nations are seriously concerned about the rising water level and the prospect of their becoming submerged.

• • •

There is no greatness where there is not simplicity, goodness, and truth.
—LEO TOLSTOY, author (1828–1910)

CHAPTER 37

Words about Words I

Search the web for "Missippi" and you'll find thousands of hits showing pages where the authors clearly meant "Mississippi." With the advent of modern computers and spell-checkers, you'd think this illustration of haplography (omission of a letter from a writing) would not occur so often. If you feel this is bad, imagine the time before the printing press came along, when the only way to make copies of a book was with a quill and parchment. Sorry, no photocopying machines to crank out double-sided copies there. Biblical translations and copies of other books from olden times are replete with haplography and its cousins. Many scholars spend their lifetime identifying these "bugs" in ancient books and other scripts.

A counterpart of haplography is haplology. Haplology occurs when one "eats" a few letters while pronouncing a word. Latin *nutrix* (nurse) came from earlier *nutritrix*. *Chancery,* a contraction of *chancellery,* is now an acceptable part of the English language. Do you think some day *probly* will be considered standard and *probably* obsolete? If there are some who economize on letters, there are others who splurge. The word for this phenomenon is *dittography* (see chapter 48). Here are a few more words about words.

haplography (hap-LOG-ruh-fee)

noun   The accidental omission of a letter or letter group that should be repeated in writing, for example, *mispell* for *misspell*. From Greek *haplo-* (single) + *-graphy* (writing).

● Robfred never missed an opportunity to profess his fondness for philology, but when he spelled it as *philogy* multiple times in the same document, it became obvious his *haplography* was not a typo.

Mississippi on Sale!

I recently discovered that if you search eBay for misspelled items, you stand an excellent chance of getting an exceptionally good deal.

There are five collectibles for "Missippi" available on eBay right now and not a single bid for any of them. If they sell at all, it will be to the unique bidder who finds them and places a lowball bid. There are 1172 items containing "Mississippi" in the title.

The same is true of "Audabon" prints. No one is bidding on them.

Once again, the economic value of correct spelling is shown—if you are a seller.

—*Peter Jennings, La Massana, Andorra*

---

obiter dictum (OB-i-tuhr DIK-tuhm), plural **obiter dicta**

noun   1. A passing comment. 2. An observation or opinion by a judge that is incidental to the case in question and not binding as precedent.

From Latin, literally, "said by the way."

• • •

I am no more humble than my talents require.
—Oscar Levant, composer (1906–1972)

● Loretta liked listening to Tolbert's keen observations, but it was his clever *obiter dicta* that swept her away.

asyndeton (uh-SIN-di-ton, -tuhn), plural **asyndeta**

noun The omission of conjunctions, as in "I came, I saw, I conquered."
From Late Latin, from Greek, from neuter of *asyndetos* (not linked), from *a-* + *syndetos* (bound together), from *syndein* (to bind together), from *syn-* + *dein* (to bind).

Asyndeton is a powerful device to indicate extemporaneous effect, and to add intensity or force to diction. Imagine if it were, "I came, I saw, and I conquered," and it's easy to see how rhythm is lost.

If you're itching to use all those conjunctions you've saved with the use of asyndeton, try polysyndeton, as in, "Uncle Jefford gobbled cookies and bagels and pizza and cake and pasta."

● While Prolixia liked to tell the story of their coming together with much detail, laconic Hector employed *asyndeton*. "We met, we engaged, we married."

verbigeration (vuhr-bij-uh-RAY-shun)

noun Obsessive repetition of meaningless words and phrases.
From Latin *verbigerare* (to talk, chat), from *verbum* (word) + *gerere* (to carry on) + *-ation*.

● Geeta knew the prime qualification to be a successful management consultant: a facility in the art of *verbigeration*.

● ● ●

It is not always the same thing to be a good man and a good citizen.
—ARISTOTLE, philosopher (384–322 B.C.E.)

brachylogy (bra–KIL–uh–jee)
noun   Conciseness of diction or an instance of such.
From Medieval Latin *brachylogia,* from Greek *brakhulogi, brakhu-,*
from *brachy-* (short) + *-logy.*

● Crocus was a busy executive, and as such he didn't have time
to speak in long form. His employees were supposed to make
sense of his *brachylogies* such as "Incentivize staff. Facilitate
transaction. Prioritize agenda."

● ● ●

Dignity consists not in possessing honors,
but in the consciousness that we deserve them.
—ARISTOTLE, philosopher (384–322 B.C.E.)

CHAPTER 38

Uncommon Words with Common Suffixes

Oniomania is another word for the urge to shop till you drop, the habit of the debit, the thrill of the bill. According to a pearl of ancient wisdom, we don't acquire things, things acquire us. In the case of oniomaniacs, it is perhaps the fun of acquiring things that acquires them. Imelda Marcos of the Philippines could be one prime example; she could also be known as a shopaholic, though she could be better known as a shoeaholic. The words collected in this chapter are uncommon words formed by common suffixes.

oniomania (O-nee-uh-MAY-nee-uh, MAYN-yuh)
noun   Excessive, uncontrollable desire to buy things.
From Latin, from Greek *onios* (for sale), derivative of *onos* (price) + *-mania* (excessive enthusiasm).

● "I did not have three thousand pairs of shoes, I had one thousand and sixty," Imelda Marcos once protested. If *oniomania* ever needs a poster girl, we know where to look.

garbology (gar-BOL-uh-jee)
noun   The study of a society or culture by examining what it discards.
From *garb*(age) + *-ology.*

● Though *garbology* remains a relatively unplumbed subject, several colleges and universities offer courses that look at what people throw away and how it reflects who they are.
　　　　　　　—*Tina Kelley, in the* New York Times *(March 23, 2000)*

onychophagia (on-i-ko-FAY-juh, -jee-uh)
noun   The practice of biting one's nails.
From Greek *onycho, onyx* (nail) + *-phagia* (eating).

● She wasn't so alarmed when she heard about Nestor's *onychophagia* until it turned out he had a preference for toenails.

philography (fi-LOG-ruh-fee)
noun   The practice of collecting autographs.
From Greek *philo-* (love) + *-graphy* (writing).

● Virtually anything to which ink will stick can be collected, swapped, or sold, according to the Universal Autograph Collectors Club, a 2,000-member association of experts in the field of *philography.*
　　　　　　　—*Ben Steelman, in* The Wilmington Morning Star
　　　　　　　　　　(October 22, 1998)

• • •

Success is not measured by the position one has reached in life,
rather by the obstacles overcome while trying to succeed.
—BOOKER T. WASHINGTON, reformer, educator, and author (1856–1915)

theophany (thee-OF-uh-nee)
noun   An appearance of a god to a person.
From Medieval Latin *theophania,* from Late Greek *theophaneia,*
Greek *theo-* (god) + *-phaneia* (showing, revelation).

● And then he had the epiphany. Wouldn't claiming to be a witness to *theophany* look good on his résumé for a career in tele-
vangelism?

• • •

Power is not revealed by striking hard or often, but by striking true.
—HONORÉ DE BALZAC, author (1799–1850)

CHAPTER 39

Words to Describe People II

The philosopher, mathematician, and writer Bertrand Russell once said, "The whole problem with the world is that fools and fanatics are always so certain of themselves, and wiser people so full of doubts." The collection of words in this chapter describes people falling somewhere in that spectrum. Can you identify some of those around you with these words?

pertinacious (pur-tn-AY-shuhs)
adjective   1. Holding resolutely to a purpose, belief, or opinion. 2. Stubbornly unyielding.
From Latin *pertinac-, pertinax, per-* (thoroughly) + *tenax* (tenacious, from *tenere* [to hold]).

● A man is *pertinacious* when he defends his folly and trusts too greatly in his own wit.
> —*Geoffrey Chaucer,* Canterbury Tales: Explicit Secunda Pars Penitentie: Part I, 1387–1400. *Translated by Walter W. Skeat.*

pixilated (PIK-suh-layt-id), also **pixillated**
adjective   1. Mentally unbalanced; eccentric. 2. Whimsical.
From *pixie,* a mischievous fairylike creature.

● He had heard of people collecting stamps, matchboxes, pens, autographs, automobiles, and the like. But rubber bands? He wondered as he browsed his *pixilated* neighbor's stretchable collection from around the world.

oscitant (OS-i-tant)
adjective   1. Yawning, gaping from drowsiness. 2. Inattentive, dull, negligent.
From Latin *oscitant,* present participle of *oscitare* (to yawn), from *os* (mouth) + *citare* (to move).

● Professor Renault's class almost always had full enrollment. If only he knew that those *oscitant* attendees were not students who had come there to learn the finer points of Kantian philosophy but local residents trying to find a cure for their insomnia.

punctilious (pungk-TIL-ee-uhs)
adjective   Extremely attentive to minute details of action or behavior.
From Italian *punctiglio,* from Spanish *puntillo,* diminutive of *punto,* from Latin *punctum* (point).

● He had come across as witty, well-informed, and sensitive during the dinner, but when he insisted on flossing before leaving for the theater, Melicia knew there wouldn't be a second date with this *punctilious* man.

● ● ●

Adults are obsolete children.
—DR. SEUSS (THEODOR GEISEL),
humorist, illustrator, and author (1904–1991)

pococurante (po-ko-koo-RAN-tee, -kyoo-)

adjective   Indifferent, apathetic, nonchalant.

noun   A careless or indifferent person.

From Italian, *poco* (little) + *curante,* present participle of *curare* (to care), from Latin, *curare, cure* (care).

● "Let them drink shakes," the *pococurante* queen replied when told the masses didn't have water to drink.

● ● ●

Oftentimes excusing of a fault/
Doth make the fault the worse by th' excuse.
—WILLIAM SHAKESPEARE, playwright and poet (1564–1616)

CHAPTER 40

Ordinal Words

"Everybody line up alphabetically according to your height." These words of Casey Stengel (1891–1975), U.S. baseball player and manager, sum up nicely the deep human need to arrange things in order, to sort, classify, and enumerate them. Here are a few phrases that characterize concepts, in descending order from fifth through first.

fifth column (fifth KOL-uhm)
noun   A group of traitors acting in sympathy with their country's enemies.
From Spanish *quinta columna* (fifth column), from the column of supporters that General Mola claimed to have in Madrid while he was leading four columns of his army to invade the city during the Spanish Civil War.

● When for the second time in a year, the plan for a secret transportation device code-named GIT, aka Plunger, was leaked to a competitor, the group of inventors was left wondering if they had a *fifth column* among them.

fourth estate (forth i-STAYT)
noun Journalistic profession; the press.
Traditionally, a power other than the three estates (the Lords Spiritual, the Lords Temporal, and the House of Commons) in the United Kingdom.

● Glismoda had great ambitions for making a career in the *fourth estate,* but she had Plan B ready—setting up a tabloid web site for publishing wild rumors—in case things didn't work out as planned.

third degree (thurd di-GREE)
noun Intensive questioning involving rough treatment.
adjective Pertaining to the third degree.
verb tr. To subject to such treatment.
There are many folk etymologies regarding possible origins of this term, but lexicographers are not certain. The more popular of the stories suggests it came from the third degree in freemasonry that was the most difficult to achieve. One aspiring to that rank was supposed to go through intense questioning and grilling.

● The police interrogators were unable to get a confession from the alleged kidnapper and knew they'd have to resort to the *third degree*—subjecting him to a nonstop stream of country music.

second fiddle (SEK-und FID-l)
noun 1. Secondary role. 2. A person in such a role.
In an orchestra, the position of concertmaster is given to the first chair violinist, who sounds the notes that all tune their instruments to, and from whom the rest of the orchestra takes their cues

● ● ●

In matters of conscience, the law of majority has no place.
—MAHATMA GANDHI, leader and social reformer (1869–1948)

any time they are playing without a conductor. So the one with second violin (second fiddle) is in a subordinate position.

The famed conductor and composer Leonard Bernstein was once asked what he thought was the most difficult instrument to play. His immediate response was, "second fiddle." He wasn't commenting on the skill required to strum second violin in an orchestra, but on the difficulty of most of us to be in the secondary role.

● "One word sums up probably the responsibility of any vice president, and that one word is to be prepared." This was how—Dan Quayle, one of the most comical vice presidents ever, explained the importance of playing *second fiddle* in the U.S. government chain of command.

first water (furst WA-tuhr)
noun   1. Formerly, the highest degree of quality in a precious stone, especially a diamond. 2. The best grade or quality.

Transparency is highly desirable in diamonds, and when they are nearly as transparent as water, they are known as diamonds of the *first water*. As the transparency decreases, we get *second* or *third water*. Hence, figuratively, something or someone of the first water is first grade, first class, or of the best in its class.

● The park ranger knew she wasn't dealing with intelligence of the *first water* when the tourist asked, "Can you tell me why so many famous Civil War battles were fought on National Park sites?"

● ● ●

The art of medicine consists in amusing the patient
while nature cures the disease.
—VOLTAIRE, philosopher (1694–1778)

CHAPTER 41

Words for Odds and Ends

S ome of the most interesting, unusual words describe everyday things. Who would have thought that the fleshy, spongy, white thing inside an orange had a word for itself . . . and that it would share this word with astronomers? Or that it would have the same ancestor as the words for an egg part, a photo book, or the smearing of a canvas? What all these words have in common is whiteness or *albus,* Latin for white. *Albumen* is egg white, an *album* is a book with white pages, and when we *daub* a sheet of paper, we de-*albus* it. Ah, the joy of words! Let's look at a few other words for odds and ends.

albedo (al–BEE–doh)
noun   1. The fraction of light reflected from a body or surface. (For example, earth's albedo is about 0.3.) 2. The white, spongy inner lining of a citrus fruit rind.
From Late Latin *albedo* (whiteness), from Latin *albus* (white).

● Rechimund had tried many ideas in the past, but he knew this time he was going to hit a jackpot—selling *albedo* extract as a nutritional supplement.

dewlap (DOO-lap, DYOO-lap)
noun A loose fold of skin hanging under the neck of an animal
such as cow, rooster, or lizard. In birds, this appendage is also
known as a wattle.
From Middle English *dewlappe: dew* (of unknown origin and
meaning) + *lap* (fold).

● "Excuse me, but is it possible to omit the *dewlaps* from the
portrait?" Herman hesitantly asked the artist he had commis-
sioned for his portrait.

chaplet (CHAP-lit)
noun 1. A wreath or garland worn on the head. 2. A string of
beads.
Middle English *chapelet* (wreath), from Old French, diminutive of
chapel (hat), from Medieval Latin *cappellus,* from Late Latin *cappa*
(cap).

● Who knew the author who appeared on *Oprah* wearing a
chaplet would launch the latest craze in headgear!

gnomon (NO-mon)
noun 1. The raised arm of a sundial that indicates the time of day
by its shadow. 2. The remaining part of a parallelogram after a similar smaller parallelogram has been taken away from one of the
corners.
From Latin *gnomon* (pointer), from Greek, from *gignoskein* (to
know).

● Eighty-six years in the making, one of the world's largest sun-
dials has finally been installed at Place de la Concorde, as part

● ● ●
A handful of sand is an anthology of the universe.
—DAVID MCCORD, poet (1897–1997)

of the Year 2000 festivities of the City of Paris. It takes an approach more cerebral than celebratory. The sundial's pointer, or *gnomon,* is the 109-foot Obelisk of Luxor. Its base is the northern half of Place de la Concorde.

—*Rose Marie Burke, in the* Wall Street Journal
(October 26, 1999)

finial (FIN-ee-ehl, FI-nee-)
noun 1. An ornamental object on top of an architectural structure or a piece of furniture. 2. A curve at the end of the main stroke of a character in some italic fonts.
From Middle English *finial* (final), from Latin *finis* (end).

● It wasn't the color or the size that she disliked about the sofa in the new apartment. But that pineapple *finial* on the sofa back had to go.

• • •

There is one art of which man should be master, the art of reflection.
—SAMUEL TAYLOR COLERIDGE, poet (1772–1834)

CHAPTER 42

Red-Herring Words

The word *sextet* has nothing to do with sex, unless of course the six people in question engage in some questionable calisthenics. That's what the English language does—often leading us on only to make things limpid in the end. There we go again. Take the word *friable,* for instance. All evidence leads us to suggest this word could be used to refer to raw potato chips. But in truth, something friable is that which could be easily crumbled. So I suppose it could be used to refer to potato chips, after all. Here are a few red-herring words, words with meanings that are not the first things that come to mind.

sextet (seks–TET)
noun   1. A group of six. 2. A group of six singers or musicians, or a piece of music composed for them.
Alteration of *sestet,* influenced by Latin *sex* (six).
   But remember, a *tenet* is not a group of ten.

● While launching his band, Ganesh considered various sizes from quartet through octet but finally settled on *sextet* for its subliminal attractive power.

potatory (POH-tuh-tor-ee)
adjective   Pertaining to or given to drinking.
From Latin *potatorius,* from Latin *potatus,* past participle of *potare* (to drink).

The word *potatory* has little to do with potatoes, unless the drink in question happens to be aquavit or poitin/poteen (an Irish moonshine). Two more familiar cousins of today's word are *potion* and *potable.*

The word *potatory* in its Latin form appears in a poem from the thirteenth-century manuscript *Carmina Burana,* attributed to goliards, a class of wandering scholar-poets. Here are the opening lines:

> Meum est propositum
> In taberna mori,
> Ut sint vina proxima
> Morientis ori.
> Tunc cantabunt laetius
> Angelorum chori:
> "Sit deus propitius
> Huic potatori!"

These lines about a drunkard's wish to die in the tavern are frequently invoked during communal acts of libation.

● Uncle Putrick's potbelly provided plentiful proof of his *potatory* pursuits.

gyrovague (JYE-ro-vayg)
noun   A monk who travels from one place to another.
From French, from Late Latin *gyrovagus, gyro-* (circle) + *vagus* (wandering).

• • •

The moment one gives close attention to anything, even a blade of grass, it becomes a mysterious, awesome, indescribably magnificent world in itself.
—HENRY MILLER, author (1891–1980)

● "Travel is fatal to prejudice, bigotry, and narrow-mindedness," Mark Twain once said. If only more people could understand the wisdom of these words, just as *gyrovagues* have.

discommode (dis–kuh–MOD)
verb tr.   To put to inconvenience.
From French *discommoder, dis-* + *commode* (convenient).

● When Gelimer's meddling neighbor knocked at the door that early morning while he was busy answering nature's call, well, let's just say he was *discommoded*.

obsequy (OB–se–kwee)
noun   A funeral rite or ceremony.
From Middle English *obsequie,* from Middle French, from Medieval Latin *obsequiae,* alteration (influenced by Latin *exsequiae,* funeral rites) of Latin *obsequia,* plural of *obsequium* (compliance).

● Filimer's bowling buddies were pleased to see his pet parrot present during the *obsequy* as per his will, but they wished he had taught the little bird fewer four-letter words.

· · ·

Ultimately, the only power to which man should aspire
is that which he exercises over himself.
—ELIE WIESEL, author and Nobel laureate (1928–)

CHAPTER 43

Discover the Theme III

It's that time again, where the theme isn't disclosed at the beginning. Instead, you the reader are challenged to discover the common thread among the words. Each word brings another clue to unravel the hidden theme. Try to find the pattern, and look for the answer on page 193.

mecca (MEK-uh)
noun   A place regarded as a center of some activity or one that many people visit.
After Mecca, a city in western Saudi Arabia, the birthplace of Muhammad and a place of pilgrimage for Muslims.

● Charcie knew where to find her ideal partner—one who could speak the Klingon language as well as she could: at a Star Trek convention, a *mecca* for science fiction buffs like her.

redd (red)
verb tr. 1. To set in order. 2. To clear.
From Middle English *redden* (to clear, to put in order).

noun   The spawning area or nest of a fish, especially a trout or a salmon.

Of unknown origin.

● "Enough messing around, now it's time to *redd* up the *redd*, dear," Mrs. Trout instructed her husband as she swam along the waves.

Mother's Always Right

Years ago, my family relocated from the heart of Pennsylvania Dutch country to Boston, where I became sensitive to my teenage friends snickering at my use of odd words. One of those words was *redd*. This is what we said to clear the dinner table. I learned not to use *redd,* but my eighty-year-old mother never did. I was delighted to tell her it was a Middle English word and she used it in the proper context after all.

—*Colleen A. Fuller, Lowell, Massachusetts*

---

ogee (oh-JEE, OH-jee)

noun   1. A curve resembling the shape of an elongated *S.* 2. An arch formed with such curves.

From Middle English *ogeus,* from Old French *ogive.*

● While he loved every inch of her, it was those cherry-red *ogees* beneath the philtrum that really charmed him. [A *philtrum* is the vertical groove below the nose.]

• • •

It is only when we forget all our learning that we begin to know.
—HENRY DAVID THOREAU, naturalist and author (1817–1862)

vug (vug, voog)

noun   A small cavity in a rock, often lined with crystals of a different mineral.

From Cornish *vooga* (cave).

● At first, the spelunker thought he had come across a clump of precious stones in the rock face. In fact, it was only a *vug* gleaming with quartz.

plica (PLY-kuh), plural **plicae** (PLI-see, -kee)

noun   1. A fold, especially of skin. 2. Hair in dirty, matted form.

From Medieval Latin, from Latin *plicare* (to fold).

● When for the third time he was implicated for removing the *plica* from the wrong knee, Dr. Dexter decided for a rather uncomplicated solution: installing a large, red, flashing neon sign in the operating room that read "Left" or "Right" as needed.

. . .

Even for our enemies in misery—there should be tears in our eyes.
—CHARAN SINGH, mystic (1916–1990)

CHAPTER 44

Newer Words in the *Oxford English Dictionary*

In the middle of 2001, the folks publishing the *Oxford English Dictionary* decided to add a few hundred words to the dictionary. That would not be newsworthy in itself—the online edition permits incorporation of new words easily, and the editors of the *OED* continually assay new words alphabetically and add them to the dictionary. What's unusual is that this time they decided to add the words out of sequence, words that otherwise would have had to wait their turn to be anointed and made part of the lexicon.

Unlike French, the English language needs no nanny's nod to call a word a word. If a word fills a need, it is a word, no matter whether it's in a dictionary. Still, the inclusion of these words in the *OED*, the most venerable dictionary around and a true lex icon, does help give writers their editors' imprimatur to use these words. As can be expected, a disproportionate number of these new words hail from the Internet. Many of these terms may appear to be slang, but we should remember that today's revolutionaries are tomorrow's conservatives. So use these words in your writing and conversation with the official seal of approval from the *OED*.

full monty (ful MON-tee), also **Full Monty, full Monty**

noun   Everything that's needed or possible or appropriate; the whole nine yards.

adjective   Complete nudity.

Origin unknown. Popularized by the 1997 movie of the same name, in which a group of unemployed steelworkers turns to stripping.

The origin of the term *full monty* isn't certain, but there is no dearth of theories. Here are some of them in decreasing order of popularity. It is quite possible one of these is true, but lexicographers have been unable to find any authoritative documentary evidence as proof:

After Field Marshal Montgomery (1887–1976):

- From his penchant for eating a full English breakfast—eggs, sausages, bacon, tomatoes, fried bread, and more (the whole enchilada?)—even while battling in the North Africa desert;

- From his habit of always showing up in full military regalia, including all his numerous medals and pins, no matter what the circumstances, hence, "showing it all," or "showing all he had";

- From his preparedness for battle and how he gave 100 percent effort;

- From his practice of going without clothes while working in his tent in North Africa's extreme heat;

• • •

Time engraves our faces with all the tears we have not shed.
—NATALIE CLIFFORD BARNEY, author (1876–1972)

- From his ordering of a previously unused style of warfare known as carpet bombing, where bombs are dropped over every bit of enemy territory, including both military and civilian areas;

- For protection and security, Montgomery would often have a double appear at functions and visits. The *full Monty* would refer to the few occasions when Montgomery himself would appear.

Other:

- From clothier Montague Burton, who advertised a complete three-piece suit;

- From demobilized British soldiers who were to collect a full set of civilian clothes from the "official" tailor on Montague Street;

- From a corruption of Monte Carlo, where *full monty* would be a big win;

- From the old European card game monte, aka three-card monte and monte bank;

- From a corruption of the phrase "the full amount";

- From the best available grade of wool, which came from South America via Montevideo;

- From an ad for Del Monte juice, which insisted on the full Del Monte;

- From the promise every now and then on *Monty Python's Flying Circus* to present "full frontal nudity."

• • •

In skating over thin ice, our safety is in our speed.
—RALPH WALDO EMERSON, philosopher and author (1803–1882)

● Grodius had been in the insurance business for too long and finally hit upon the idea of launching the *full monty* of insurance policies: one that insured against falling meteorites, alien invasion, and the flooding of Earth, among other more mundane matters such as dental decay.

bad hair day (bad hair day)

noun   A day when everything seems to go wrong.

Extension of the literal meaning of the term *bad hair day,* a day when one's hair is, well, hairy.

● His pet hamster ran away, he received an IRS audit notice in the mail, and then he hit a lawyer's Mercedes on his way to work... sounds like Matrus was having a *bad hair day.*

nutraceutical (noo-truh-SOO-ti-kuhl)

noun   A food with (or believed to have) medicinal properties.

adjective   Pertaining to nutraceuticals.

Blend of the words *nutrient* and *pharmaceutical.*

● It came to him in a dream, the idea of the perfect *nutraceutical,* and he knew he had to make it a reality: combining chihuahua cartilage, root of amaranth, yellow-green algae, and water from the Dead Sea.

retail therapy (REE-tayl THER-uh-pee)

noun   Shopping as a means of comfort, relaxation, or cheering up.

● Mrs. McDrus is at Bloomingdale's doing her *retail therapy* right now. May I take a message for her?

● ● ●

A real patriot is the fellow who gets a parking ticket
and rejoices that the system works.
—BILL VAUGHAN, journalist (1915–1977)

webliography (web–lee–OG–ruh–fee)
noun   A list of electronic documents on a particular topic.
Blend of the words *web* and *bibliography*.

- Dandruth's penchant for tying eclectic subjects together was amply demonstrated in the *webliography* for his term paper that included links to sites related to lacrosse rules, the Llama Farmers' Association, the White House, and the Panama Canal.

. . .

Library: A place where the dead lie.
—ELBERT HUBBARD, author, editor, and printer (1856–1915)

CHAPTER 45

War of Words and Words of War

O ne more such victory and we are lost," exclaimed Pyrrhus, the king of Epirus, as he described his costly success in the battle of Asculum in Apulia. With these words he gave us a metaphor to refer to a victory so costly that it's hardly better than defeat. Yet, if we talk to those who lost their sons, husbands, or fathers to war, every victory is a pyrrhic victory. A war is perhaps the only occasion when killing a person is not only accepted but rewarded. If only we could learn to do war with words instead. Till then, let's look at a few words of war.

pyrrhic victory (PIR-ik VIK-tuh-ree)
noun   A victory won at too great a cost.
After Pyrrhus, the king of Epirus, who suffered staggering losses while defeating Romans.

- Courts in many countries, such as India, are notorious for delay. It may sound mind-boggling, but a case can last decades, even several generations. No wonder the winner feels like she has won a *pyrrhic* victory.

When a War Produced a Saint

After knowing this word, the immediate example, from this part of the world (India), that came to my mind is the (in)famous victory of King Ashoka over Kalinga in 262 B.C. After the victory, the king felt so *pyrrhic* (!) about it that he almost became a saint, following Buddhism.

—*P.K. Venkataraghavan, Bangalore, India*

Pyrrhic victory reminded me of the comment made by Prince Bernhard of the Netherlands after Field Marshal Montgomery had said of the ill-fated Operation Market-Garden (the Battle of Arnhem, September 1944) that he remained an unrepentant advocate of it. Bernhard said, "My country can never again afford the luxury of another Montgomery success." (Quoted by Cornelius Ryan in *A Bridge Too Far*)

—*Byron Gassman, Orem, Utah*

casus belli (KAY-suhs BEL-y, BEL-ee), plural **casus belli**
noun   An action or event that causes or is used to justify starting a war.
From New Latin *casus belli,* from Latin *casus* (occasion), *belli,* genitive of *bellum* (war).

● Glindus knew he could afford everything but forgetting their wedding anniversary—that would be a *casus belli* in the family.

fetial (FEE-shuhl), also **fecial**
adjective   Relating to declarations of war and treaties of peace.
From Latin *fetialis,* a member of the Roman college of priests, who performed the rites in such matters.

• • •

When I play with my cat,
who knows whether I do not make her more sport than she makes me?
—MICHEL DE MONTAIGNE, essayist (1533–1592)

- Little Irfan's command of the *fetial* arts in settling playground fistfights gave his parents hope that one day he was going to be a major world leader.

polemology (po-luh-MOL-uh-jee)
noun   The science and study of human conflict and war.
From Greek *polemos* (war) + *-logy.* The word *polemic* shares the same root.

- Janthrus had worked in conflict resolution among teens in the past and that sounded like the perfect preparation for her future job in the United Nations center for *polemology.* After all, nations fight over more or less the same stuff as teens: ego, whim, money, and things.

spoliation (spo-lee-AY-shun)
noun   1. The act of pillaging, plundering, or spoiling. 2. Seizure of neutral ships at sea in time of war. 3. The deliberate destruction or alteration of a document.
From Middle English, from Latin *spoliatus,* past participle of *spoliare* (spoil, lay waste).

- Bombs are agnostic, impartial, and indifferent. When they explode, their *spoliation* doesn't discriminate whether one is Hindu or Christian, saint or sinner, aged or infant; they just do their job.

• • •

Access to power must be confined to those who are not in love with it.
—PLATO, philosopher (427–347 B.C.E.)

CHAPTER 46

Words for Physical Characteristics Used to Describe People Figuratively

A popular admonition goes, "Don't judge a book by its cover." Yet we do it all the time. We ascribe qualities of character to people based on their physical characteristics. And our language takes shape to reflect that attitude. Are cross-eyed people shady? I don't think so. At least not any more than the straight-eyed ones. Let's take a look at more such words.

louche (loosh)
adjective   Of questionable character; dubious; disreputable.
From French *louche* (cross-eyed), from Old French *lousche*, feminine of *lois,* from Latin *lusca,* feminine of *luscus* (one-eyed).

- The handsome man she met at the party was charming and funny, yet she couldn't help noticing something *louche* about him.

A Parisian Slang

The suffix *-ard* is even more fun in French. It's a derogatory suffix in French slang that gets applied to many words to modify them, usually into insults. For instance, while *chauffeur* in French means *driver*—not just the limo kind; *chauffeur de taxi* means simply *taxi driver*—*chauffard* is slang for someone who drives badly. A common mild expletive is *espece de chauffard!*—literally, "species of bad driver"—which you can say anytime someone cuts you off or sits in front of you when the light turns green.

        —*James Bradley, Los Angeles, California*

---

clochard (KLOH-shahr)
noun A beggar; vagrant.
From French *clocher* (to limp), from Latin *clopus* (lame).

- When she visited New York City for the first time, the contrast was too strong for her to ignore: multimillion-dollar condos juxtaposed with *clochards* with nothing to call a home.

myopic (my-OP-ik)
adjective 1. Nearsighted; unable to see clearly objects at a distance. 2. Shortsighted; lacking foresight; narrow-minded.
From New Latin, from Greek *myopia,* from *myop-* (nearsighted), from *myein* (to close) + *ops* (eye).

• • •

In the presence of eternity, the mountains are as transient as the clouds.
—ROBERT GREEN INGERSOLL, lawyer and orator (1833–1899)

● Always *myopic,* in the age of word-processing Grunthus put his money in a typewriter company.

dexterous (DEK-struhs, -stuhr-uhs) also **dextrous**
adjective 1. Skillful or adroit, mentally or bodily. 2. Right-handed. From Latin *dexter* (right-hand, skillful).

● *Dexterous* Demeter's favorite pastime during his commute was solving Rubik's Cube with one hand while steering the car with the other.

Left-Handed but Right-Minded
Dexterous is yet another example of the tyranny of the majority, right-handers presuming to be more adroit (French, "to the right") than lefties. It's been said that if the left side of the brain controls the right side of the body, then only left-handed people are in their right minds.
— *William S. Haubrich, M.D., La Jolla, California*

---

ambisinister (am-bi-SIN-uh-stuhr)
adjective Clumsy with both hands. (Literally, "with two left hands.") Latin *ambi-* (both) + *sinister* (on the left side).

● Staff sergeant Gawkward hoped to win a medal or two by firing two rifles at the same time. When he managed to hit his fellow soldiers instead, all he earned was the remark *"ambisinister"* in his service record.

• • •
The highest purpose is to have no purpose at all.
This puts one in accord with nature in her manner of operation.
—JOHN CAGE, composer (1912–1992)

Words Politicians Play With

The words *sinister* and *ambisinister* reminded me of a quip attributed to one of our more famous prime ministers, the late Pierre Elliot Trudeau. Following a particularly long-winded speech in parliament by a socialist member, Mr. Trudeau rose and said simply, "How fortunate we are in this country, Mr. Speaker, that the left is more gauche than sinister."

—*Paddy Hernon, Victoria, B.C., Canada*

• • •

Sometimes to remain silent is to lie.
—MIGUEL DE UNAMUNO, philosopher and author (1864–1936)

CHAPTER 47

Words Evolved from Folk Etymologies

An e-mail titled "Life in the 1500s" has been making the rounds of the Internet for quite some time. This piece of creative writing purports to depict life at the time of Shakespeare and his wife Ann Hathaway and to explain the origins of many popular idioms. While this forwarded e-mail makes fascinating reading, it's simply a product of some netter's wild imagination. It's a shining example of folk etymologies: popular stories about the origins of words that sound convincing but aren't necessarily true.

On the other hand, there are cases when a mistaken assumption about the origin or meaning of a word does result in a change in its form. The word *shamefaced* evolved from Middle English *shamefast* (modest, shy) and had nothing to do with the face. The similarity of pronunciations of *fast* and *faced* made some mistake the sound and we got *shamefaced*. Here are some other examples.

humble pie (HUM-buhl pi)

noun Humiliation in the form of apology or retraction. Often in form of the phrase "to eat humble pie."

From the phrase *an umble pie,* transformed by folk etymology by resemblance to the word *humble.* The phrase *an umble pie* itself was made by false splitting *from a numble pie. Numbles* or *nombles* are edible animal entrails. The words came to us from Latin via French.

● His prediction that the Internet would crash under its own weight turned out not to be true, and the magazine columnist was forced to eat *humble pie.*

kickshaw (KIK-shaw)

noun 1. A fancy dish; delicacy. 2. A trinket.

By folk etymology, from French *quelque chose* (something).

● The credit card company offered a *kickshaw* for free to their cardholders as a token of gratitude for being their valuable customers. One only had to pay a small shipping and handling charge which, incidentally, just happened to be around the price of the trinket offered.

wiseacre (WIZ-ay-kuhr)

noun One who obnoxiously pretends to be wise; smart aleck; wise guy.

From Middle Dutch *wijsseg, gher* (soothsayer), translation of Middle High German *wissage,* from Old High German *wissago* (wise person), altered by folk etymology.

● During the cross-examination, when the lawyer asked if she had lived in the town all her life, the *wiseacre* witness replied, "Not yet."

● ● ●

As great scientists have said and as all children know, it is above all by the imagination that we achieve perception, and compassion, and hope.
—URSULA LE GUIN, author (1929–)

rakehell (RAYK-hel)
noun   A licentious or immoral person.
By folk etymology from Middle English *rakel* (rash, hasty).

● Fred the *rakehell* quietly smiled as he read the biographies of the famous presidents. At least he had something in common with them.

chaise longue (shayz LONG), plural **chaise longues** or **chaises longues** (shays LONG)
noun   A reclining chair with an elongated seat for supporting legs.
From French (literally, long chair). The prevalent variant form of this term, *chaise lounge,* is formed by folk etymology.

● And then Dorian heaved contentedly as he pondered how little one needs if one lives simply, maybe just a comfortable *chaise longue* and a big-screen TV.

• • •

Reject your sense of injury and the injury itself disappears.
—MARCUS AURELIUS, philosopher and author (121–180)

CHAPTER 48

Words about Words II

Every year, in early April, followers of the Shia sect of Muslims take part in elaborate processions commemorating sacrifices of Husain, grandson of the Prophet Muhammad. They beat their chests with fists and iron chains as a mark of penance while chanting, "Ya Hasan! Ya Husain!" To a native English speaker, those cries perhaps sound more like "Hobson-Jobson." So in 1886, when Henry Yule, a member of the British government in India, published a book of anglicized colloquial words from Indian languages, he chose that very expression as the title for his collection: *Hobson-Jobson*. And ever since we refer to that process and the words thus formed by the same name.

This process of lexical and phonological assimilation of words from one language to another is not confined to any particular set of languages. We see this mix of pun and folk etymology whenever speakers of two diverse languages cross paths. You may have heard about "Harry Kerry," the preferred method of suicide by Japanese warriors. Here are other examples:

juggernaut from Sanskrit *Jagannatha*
plonk (cheap wine) from French [vin] *blanc*

> *Mary Jane/Mary Warner/Mary Jane Warner* for Mexican/Spanish
>   *marijuana*
> *hocus-pocus* from Latin *hoc est corpus*

You can find the delightful *Hobson-Jobson* dictionary in your library, or browse through it on the Web at http://bibliomania.com/ 2/3/260/. While you are there, don't forget to look up *puggry*. (It's the answer to a very popular puzzle: Find a word ending in *-gry* besides *hungry* and *angry*.)

Hobson-Jobson (HOB-suhn JOB-suhn)

noun   Adaptation of a foreign word or phrase to fit the sound and spelling patterns of the borrowing language.

From the title of an 1886 book of the same name.

● Rushdie's characters talk like Wodehouse characters playing with *Hobson-Jobson:* "In this God-fearing Christian house, British still is best, madder-moyselle.... If you have ambitions in our boy's direction, then please to mindofy your mouth."
>   —*James Wood, in* The New Republic *(March 18, 1996)*

Hobson-Jobson Galore

My favorite is Cuba and other Latin countries where a baseball "home run" is a *jonron*, pronounced "hon-ron."
>   —*Steve Benko, Southport, Connecticut*

One way of pluralizing a noun in Hebrew is by the addition of the syllable (transliterated) *-im* at the end. Thus arose the early term (and terrible pun) for automobile headlights when modern Hebrew found itself without a word for them. Taking a cue from one of the then-current brands of American headlights, Sealed Beam, the Hebrew simply took

---

• • •

They also serve who only stand and wait.
—JOHN MILTON, poet (1608–1674)

this as a ready-made plural, and made it *silbim*. I don't believe I ever heard the singular, which would be *silb*, and am
pretty sure that the plural itself has now been supplanted by
a noun more honorably derived.

—*Robert Richter, M.D., New York City, New York*

Here in New Zealand, there are plentiful examples of
Hobson-Jobson phrases and words—the most well-known
internationally probably being *taboo*, from the general Poly-
nesian word *tapu*, meaning "sacred."

—*James Dignan (grutness@surf4nix.com)*

In Costa Rica we have innumerable Hobson-Jobsons: *canfin*—
for *kerosene*—taken from the grade "candle fine"; we love eating *queque* (pronounced "kay-kay")—*cake* for dessert; while in
Colombia they have a delicious cake called *ponqué—pound
cake*. And in Puerto Rico many people use fifty-five gallon
drums as garbage cans, they are called a *safacón* (a safety can).
In general, Spanish is rife with this type of adoption; we really
do enjoy a "cultural interchange" with English, which has
adopted so many words from Spanish.

—*Marcos Bogan, Miami, Florida*

I'm in Bogotá, Colombia, and here Hobson-Jobson is a
really serious topic. The Real Academia (royal academy),
which attempts to regulate the Spanish language, has a lot
of difficulty with English words that have been adopted
into Spanish by the common people. A few years ago they
finally accepted *sweater* and *sandwich*. Only, for the sake of
maintaining the phonetic rules of Spanish (which make
spoken and written Spanish a closer match than spoken and
written English) they changed the spellings to *sueter* and
sanduche respectively.

—*Ted Zuur, Bogotá, Colombia*

• • •

You cannot shake hands with a clenched fist.
—INDIRA GANDHI, Indian prime minister (1917–1984)

> My grandmom's favourite scolding is "O plus." For a very
> very long time, since my childhood, I've wondered what
> she could possibly mean by calling the milkman or the veg-
> etable vendor or one of us, when we've been naughty, O+.
> Till I realized she actually meant *hopeless!*
>
> —*Deepa Duraiswamy, India*

dittography (di-TOG-ruh-fee)

noun   The inadvertent repetition of letters, syllables, words, or
phrases in
in writing.
From Greek *ditto* (double) + *-graphy* (writing).

● When little Garth spelled the word *remember* as *rememember* for
the nth time, his teacher sent a note to his parents, "Please remember to work with him to remedy the *dittography* in his or-
thography."

eye dialect (eye-DY-uh-lekt)

noun   Unusual or nonstandard spelling to represent an unedu-
cated or youthful speaker or to convey dialectal or colloquial
speech.
Examples: *wuz* (was), *enuff* (enough), *warez* (wares), *peepul* (people).
    First used in print by George Phillip Krapp (1872–1934) in
The English Language in America to denote spellings in which "the
convention violated is one of the eyes, not of the ear."

· · ·

Let us so live that when we come to die even the undertaker will be sorry.
—MARK TWAIN, author and humorist (1835–1910)

● Grundus used *eye dialect* to convey a southern setting in his latest novel. A character calls tech support and says, "Yeah, WINDAS on mah computa ain't workin'."

epenthesis (uh-PEN-thu-sis)
noun   Insertion of an extra sound into a word, e.g., *fillum* for *film*. From Late Latin, from Greek *epentithenai* (to insert), from *ep-, epi-,* (in addition) + *en-* (in) *thesis* (setting, placement), stem of *tithenai* (to put).

● Timgruf had called his host ahead to get the directions, but when he couldn't find Ellum Street even after spending hours driving in the area, he realized he had been a victim of *epenthesis.*

Noam Chomsky or Nim Chimpsky?
Epenthesis is responsible for the *p* in *Thompson,* originally "Thomas's son." One example of epenthesis cited by the preeminent linguist Noam Chomsky was his own last name, generally pronounced as if it were spelled "chomp-sky." In honor of Dr. Chomsky, one of the chimps at one of the labs where they were trying to teach chimps sign language was named Nim Chimpsky. The pun was a fitting tribute!

—Maureen Roult, Hyattsville, Maryland

My husband is originally from Lithuania. Most Americans make it an epenthesis when they pronounce it Lith-a-uania! But my all-time favorites are real-a-tor, nuc-u-lar, and ath-a-lete!

—Vicky Tarulis, Fountain Hills, Arizona

● ● ●

We are so vain that we even care for the opinion of those we don't care for.
—MARIE VON EBNER-ESCHENBACH, writer (1830–1916)

idiolect (ID-ee-uh-lekt)
noun   Language usage pattern unique to a person.
From Greek *idio-* (personal, peculiar) + *dialect* (language unique to a group of people).

● When her kindergarten teacher corrected her again on what he believed was her non-standard diction, Aurelia protested, "But that's my *idiolect*."

• • •
Nothing so soon the drooping spirits can raise /
As praises from the men, whom all men praise.
—ABRAHAM COWLEY, poet (1618–1667)

CHAPTER 49

Words Formed Using Combining Forms

It's a good thing we don't have to act out the literal meaning of words or we'd all be exercising in the nude in gymnasia. The word *gymnasium* comes to us from the Greek *gymnazein*, literally, to train in the nude. Other words formed using the combining form *gymno-* (naked or bare) are *gymnoplast* (a protoplasm without a surrounding wall) and *gymnosophy* (a form of philosophy practiced by a sect of ascetics who refuse to wear clothes).

As its name indicates, a combining form is a linguistic form that combines with a free word or another combining form to make a word. Sometimes there can be two combining forms joining a third *(auto-bio-graphy)*. Also the same combining form can take different positions at different times *(-graph-* in *graphology* and *autograph)*. Then there are instances where the same combining form can join itself to produce a word *(logology,* the study of words). All this can perhaps be explained very well using humans as the metaphor. But as this book is family-oriented, we'll resist that temptation. Instead, let's take a look at some unusual words formed by other combining forms: *miso-* (hate), *pili-* (hair), *ichno-* (track), *stego-* (cover), and *chiro-* (hand).

misocainea (mis-oh–KY-nee-uh, mi-soh–)

noun   Hatred of anything new.
From Greek *miso-* (hate) + *kainos* (new).

● The selection committee knew they had found the perfect candidate for the post of museum curator when they came across the mention of *misocainea* in Sunilda's resume.

piliform (PIL-i-form)

adjective   Having the form of a hair.
From Neo-Latin *piliformis,* from *pili-* (hair) + *-form.*

● Barbara was known for her unusual culinary arrangements, and her latest was an elaborate *piliform* pasta dish.

ichnology (ik-NOL-uh–jee)

noun   A branch of paleontology dealing with the study of fossilized footprints, tracks, or traces.
From *ichno-* (track or footstep) + *-logy* (study).

● Little Pumpernickel could recognize the brand of a shoe just by looking at the footprints, to the delight of her proud parents, who saw a budding *ichnology* expert in her.

steganography (ste-guh–NOG-ruh–fee)

noun   Secret communication by hiding the existence of a message.
From Greek *stego-* (cover) + *-graphy* (writing).

• • •

Support the strong, give courage to the timid,
remind the indifferent, and warn the opposed.
—WHITNEY M. YOUNG, social worker and educator (1921–1971)

A few examples of *steganography:* shrinking the secret text repeatedly until it's the size of a dot and then putting it in an unsuspected place, such as on top of a letter *i* in some innocuous letter. Second, shaving the head of a man, writing the secret message on his pate with unwashable ink, and then letting the hair grow back before dispatching him to the destination. To take an example from modern digital techniques, one could put the text of a message in the least significant bits in an image file. A number of steganography software programs are available on the Internet for free or at very little cost.

So what is the difference between cryptography and steganography? The former encrypts the message, while the latter hides the message altogether. So while use of cryptography might raise the suspicion that something secret is being communicated, in steganography one employs an innocuous message to send the hidden message.

Here is a little joke with a fine example of steganography.

- A memo from a manager with a recommendation for an employee:

Bob Smith, an assistant programmer, can always be found
hard at work in his cubicle. Bob works independently, without
wasting company time talking to colleagues. Bob never
thinks twice about assisting fellow employees, and he always
finishes given assignments on time. Often Bob takes extended
measures to complete his work, sometimes skipping
coffee breaks. Bob is a dedicated individual who has absolutely no
vanity in spite of his high accomplishments and profound
knowledge in his field. I firmly believe that Bob can be
classed as a high-caliber employee, the type that cannot be

• • •

Shall I tell you the secret of the true scholar? It is this: every man
I meet is my master in some point, and in that I learn of him.
—RALPH WALDO EMERSON, philosopher and author (1803–1882)

dispensed with. Consequently, I duly recommend that Bob be promoted to executive management, and a proposal will be sent away as soon as possible.

A second memo clarifies that Bob Smith was reading over the manager's shoulder while that recommendation letter was being written, and that only alternate lines of the previous communication should be considered.

chiromancy (KY-ruh-man-see)
noun   The practice of predicting character and life of a person from the lines on the palms; palmistry.
From Greek *chiro-* (hand) + *-mancy* (divination).

● According to *chiromancy* experts, the palms of a person are an accurate record of her past, present, and future.

• • •

It is the characteristic of the most stringent censorships
that they give credibility to the opinions they attack.
—VOLTAIRE, philosopher (1694–1778)

CHAPTER 50

Toponyms, or Words Derived from Place Names

Known to the ancients as the northernmost region of the habitable world, Thule has been variously identified as one of the Shetland Islands, Norway, or Iceland. Today's Thule is in northwest Greenland, within the Arctic Circle.

Incidentally, the name Greenland is ironic, as more than four-fifths of the land is ice-capped. The palindromically named village of Qaanaaq, in the district of Thule, has the distinction of being the northernmost naturally inhabited place on earth.

Let's visit a few words that take their names from faraway places in both fact and fiction.

ultima Thule (UL-tuh-muh THOO-lee)
noun   1. The northernmost part of the world believed habitable by the ancients. 2. A distant or remote goal or place.
From Latin *ultima* (farthest), *Thule* (name of a place).

● McFrud traveled to the *ultima Thule* in search of peace before he realized it was within him.

El Dorado (el doh–RAH–doh)

noun 1. A legendary place in South America sought for its treasures by sixteenth-century explorers. 2. A place offering fabulous wealth or opportunity.

From Spanish, literally, "the gilded one."

● The Gold Rush of the late 1990s had people flocking to the stock market *El Dorado,* only to discover it was all fool's gold.

Timbuktu (tim–buk–TOO)

noun 1. The name of a city on the edge of the Sahara Desert in central Mali (West Africa). 2. Any remote, inaccessible place.

● He loved working in the busy downtown except that he had to park in *Timbuktu.*

stoic (STOH–ik)

noun One who is or appears to be indifferent to pleasure or pain; unaffected by emotions.

adjective Unaffected by pleasure or pain.

After the name of the school of philosophy founded by Greek philosopher Zeno (c. 340–265 B.C.E.) that one should be free of passion and be unaffected by grief or joy.

From Middle English, from Latin *stoicus,* from Greek *stoikos* from *stoa* (the porch where Zeno taught).

● He had seen the world and at his ripe age, he remained *stoic* in the face of the ups and downs of life.

• • •

Bed is the poor man's opera.
—ITALIAN PROVERB

brigadoon (BRIG-uh-doon)
noun   An idyllic place that is out of touch with reality or one that makes its appearance for a brief period in a long time.
From *Brigadoon,* a village in the musical of the same name, by Alan Jay Lerner and Frederick Loewe, based on the story *Germelshausen* by Friedrich Gerstacker. Brigadoon is under a spell that makes it invisible to outsiders except on one day every 100 years.

● McDearths, having lived in the hullabaloo of New York City for too long, was only too happy to move to a *brigadoon,* a pastoral trailer community in the middle of nowhere in North Dakota.

• • •

Laws are the spider's webs which, if anything small falls into them they ensnare it, but large things break through and escape.
—SOLON, statesman (c. 638–c. 558 B.C.E.)

CHAPTER 51

Words for Body Parts That Are Used Metaphorically

Ever met a woman who gave her heart away and yet didn't turn heartless? Or a man of short physique who was still bighearted? Wonder how we may have a change of heart without ever having to go to a heart surgeon? There are people one could call lion-hearted, or those who have a chicken heart, yet they have never had heart replacement surgery. There are times when we are warmhearted, and on other occasions we might act with a cold heart, without any reference to our body temperature. We may come across a bleeding heart yet never call a cardiologist. Oh, how we use our heart as the metaphor for actions, emotions, intentions, and feelings!

And the heart is not the only part of anatomy we use in this way. Here are a few words for body parts that are used metaphorically.

visceral (VIS-er-uhl)

adjective   1. Related to viscera. 2. Instinctive, not reasoning or in-tellectual. 3. Dealing with base emotions; earthy, crude.

From Medieval Latin *visceralis,* from Latin *viscera* (internal organs), plural of *viscus* (flesh). From the belief that viscera were the seat of emotions.

● Helms will not remain to torment his legions of enemies. But the *visceral* brand of politics he pioneered will probably never go away.

           —*Eleanor Clift, in* Newsweek *(September 3, 2001)*

liverish (LIV-er-ish)

adjective   1. Resembling liver, especially in color. 2. Ill-natured, grouchy.

From Middle English, Old English *lifer* + *-ish.* From the former belief that such a disposition was a symptom of excess secretion of bile owing to liver disorder.

● No matter how *liverish* he was feeling, one look at his pet iguana and Laffwell would be his cheerful self again.

adrenalize (a-DREEN-uh-lyz)

verb   To excite and stir to action.

From *adrenaline,* a hormone produced by adrenal glands (above the kidneys), secreted when a person is excited. From Latin *renes* (kidney).

● The most adventurous thing he had done so far was riding an escalator without his hands on the railing, and the idea of

● ● ●

Applause is the spur of noble minds, the end and aim of weak ones.
—CHARLES CALEB COLTON, author (1780–1832)

bungee-jumping from a 100-foot bridge *adrenalized* him, to say the least.

phlegmatic (fleg-MAT-ik)

adjective   Having a sluggish temperament; apathetic. 2. Calm or composed.

From Middle English *fleumatike,* from Old French *fleumatique,* from Late Latin *phlegmaticus,* from Greek *phlegmatikos,* from the humor *phlegm,* from *phlegein* (to burn). From *phlegm,* one of the four body humors, ascribed to these qualities.

● The usually *phlegmatic* Uncle Cliveship had a fond relationship with his model 1968 Ford, and in general his temperament could be accurately predicted by the state of the functioning of the automobile.

jugular (JUG-uh-luhr)

adjective   Of or pertaining to the neck or throat.

noun 1. A jugular vein. 2. The most important or vulnerable part of something.

From Late Latin *jugularis,* from Latin *jugulum* (collarbone, throat), from Latin *jugum* (yoke).

● Fritigern figured highlighting his go-for-the-*jugular* approach couldn't hurt as he prepared his résumé for the position of an aggressive marketing manager advertised in the local newspaper.

● ● ●

In nature there are neither rewards nor punishments;
there are consequences.
—ROBERT GREEN INGERSOLL, lawyer and orator (1833–1899)

CHAPTER 52

Red-Herring Words Revisited

Here is a pop quiz: How many light-years does it take for an astronomer to change a lightbulb? The answer, of course, is none. She knows a light-year is a unit of distance, not time. The red-herring word *year* in this term tries to mislead us. This chapter brings together words whose meanings are not the first thing that comes to mind.

debridement (di–BREED–ment, day–)
noun Surgical removal of dead, infected tissue or foreign matter from a wound.
From French *debridement,* from *debrider* (to unbridle), from Middle French *desbrider (de- + brider).*

- Alan's stories of getting wounded in the war and the subsequent *debridement* of the debris moved his listeners to tears.

escheat (es–CHEET)
noun 1. The reversion of property to the state or crown in case of no legal heirs. 2. Property that has reverted to the state or crown.

verb tr. and intr.   To revert or cause to revert property.
From Middle English *eschete,* from Old French *eschete,* from Vulgar
Latin *excadere,* from Latin *ex-* + *cadere* (to fall).

● The state of Exadonia was lurching towards deficit financing
when the representatives came up with the clever idea of re-
ducing the time before the state *escheats* abandoned property.

Death Warrant
Escheat is a word that used to crop up relatively frequently
in Scots legal usage, although not so much these days. In
particular, I was reminded of the old form of death warrant
issued by Scots courts when a prisoner was sentenced to
death. My father used to work at the High Court of Justi-
ciary in Edinburgh (the Supreme Criminal Court of Scotland) and came across an old death warrant at the back of
one of the stationery cupboards. Such a warrant would have
been signed by the judge after pronouncing sentence of
death, something done whilst the judge wore his "doom-
ster" cap (a black cap). The terms of the death sentence,
narrated on the warrant, included the penalty that the con-
demned prisoner's goods were forfeit and "escheat" to the
Crown. Rather a sinister use of the word, but of interest
nonetheless!
—*Martin Hogg, Edinburgh, Scotland*

---

antiphony (an-TIF-uh-nee)
noun   Responsive alternation between two groups, especially between singers.
From *antiphon* (a song sung in alternate parts), from Middle English, from Greek *antiphona.*

• • •
What is to give light must endure burning.
—VIKTOR FRANKL, author, neurologist, psychiatrist,
and Holocaust survivor (1905–1997)

● Jill and her husband loved singing and delighted in quotidian sessions of *antiphony.*

limpid (LIM–pid)
adjective   1. Clear; transparent. 2. Easily comprehensible; clear. 3. Calm; serene.
From Latin *limpidus* (clear).

● Gulherd had a way with words, and his *limpid* prose transformed even the mundane description of hauling out the trash into poetry.

In his unusual recipe collection *The Gentleman's Companion,* Charles H. Baker Jr. talks about sauteing onions "until they are limpid as a maiden's eye and tender as her loving glance."

sexcentenary (seks–sen–TEN–uh–ree)
adjective   Relating to the number 600 or a period of 600 years.
noun   A 600th anniversary.
From Latin *sex* (six) + *centenary* (a period of 100 years), from *centenarius.*

● On the historic milestone, the enthusiastic reverend invited the parish to celebrate the *sexcentenary* at the place of worship, but he wasn't sure why he received so many angry responses.

● ● ●

You can't turn back the clock. But you can wind it up again.
—BONNIE PRUDDEN, fitness trainer and author (1914–)

CHAPTER 53

Words from Nature's Oeuvre

Who knows how large the universe is? A few years ago, it was estimated that there are more than 150 billion galaxies in the universe, and the number is still growing. Assuming there is life only on Earth (a big assumption), for a population of six billion there are 25 galaxies per person. Nature has provided for everyone abundantly.

Just on Earth—a tiny speck in this universe—there are countless delights for us to explore. Here, we feature five words from nature's oeuvre.

fjord (fyord), also **fiord**
noun   A long, narrow inlet of sea between steep cliffs, often formed by glacial action.
From Norwegian *fjord,* from Old Norse *fjorthr.*

● *Fjords* were formed when glaciers carved deep valleys in the mountains, which were eventually filled with salt water from the sea.

estuary (ES-choo-er-ee)

noun   The body of water formed where the fresh water of a river meets salt water of an ocean.

From Latin *aestuarium* (channel, inlet), from *aestus* (surge, tide).

● The unique environment of *estuaries* provides a habitat to a variety of species of plants and animals.

peninsula (peh-NIN-su-lah)

noun   A piece of land that juts out in the water and is connected to the larger body, usually by an isthmus.

From Latin *paeninsula,* from *paene* (almost) + *insula* (island).

● The meeting place of Europe and Africa, the Iberian *Peninsula* is separated from the rest of Europe by the Pyrenees mountain range and from Africa by the Strait of Gibraltar.

archipelago (ar-kih-PEL-uh-go)

noun   A group of islands or a part of a sea with a group of islands.

From Italian *arcipelago,* from Greek *arkhi-* (chief, main) + *pelagos* (sea).

The term was first used to refer to the Aegean Sea, an arm of the Mediterranean Sea between Greece and Turkey. If you see it on the map, you will see a large number of islands in the area.

● Mountains under water? The Alexander *Archipelago* is a group of more than 1,000 islands off southeastern Alaska. These heavily forested islands are, in fact, the exposed tops of submerged coastal mountains in the Pacific Ocean.

● ● ●

The road uphill and the road downhill are one and the same.
—HERACLITUS, philosopher (c. 540–470 B.C.E.)

massif (ma-SEEF)

noun   A compact mountain mass with one or more summits.
From French *massif* (massive, solid). Originally this word in French
was specifically used to refer to the Massif Central, the mountain-
ous area in southern central France.

● Vinson *Massif,* Antarctica's highest peak, is named after Carl G.
Vinson, a U.S. congressman who lobbied the U.S. government
for exploration of Antarctica.

• • •

Work saves us from three great evils: boredom, vice and need.
—VOLTAIRE, philosopher (1694–1778)

CHAPTER 54

Words about People Who Love Books

So many books, so little time! Do you find yourself muttering these words as you browse the shelves in a library or a bookstore? Rest assured, you are not alone in your love of books. It was the Dutch writer Desiderius Erasmus who said, "When I get a little money I buy books; and if any is left I buy food and clothes." This fondness for books spans a wide range. At the extreme, the urge to acquire books has been ascribed as the motive behind murders. Don Vicente, a Spaniard, killed as many as eight people to acquire a book in 1836. And there have been thieves who find the only valuables are books and therefore steal only books. Stephen Blumberg of the United States, for example, stole precious books worth millions of dollars from hundreds of university libraries during the 1970s and 1980s, all for his own pleasure, not for resale.

We've arranged the words in this chapter in order of increasing degree of affinity for books. So leaf through these words and find out where your bibliomania falls within this spectrum. As the experiences related here show, the love of books knows no boundary. From San Francisco to Sydney, the feeling is identical, varying only in degree, not in kind.

Who Am I?
Would you call it *bibliomania* when one has books in every single room, on shelves, on floors and on the sofa, in the kitchen on the microwave oven and in the car? Reading several books at the same time? Not being able to resist acquiring books if I make the mistake of entering a bookstore? It is like shopping in supermarket, do not go in when hungry.

—*Phillippa Cribb, Hamburg, Germany*

---

bibliophage (BIB-lee-uh-fayj)
noun   A bookworm, literally "one who eats books."
From Greek *biblio-* (book) + *-phage* (one that eats).

● Clia, the *bibliophage,* wasn't too worried when she discovered she was locked in the library at closing time.

bibliophile (BIB-lee-uh-fyl), also **bibliophil** (-fil) or **bibliophilist** (bib-lee-OF-uh-list)
noun   A book lover.
From Greek *biblio-* (book) + *-phile* (lover of).

● When her friend suggested that she give a book to her *bibliophile* husband on his birthday, Vanessa replied, "He already has one."

• • •

Pleasure is very seldom found where it is sought; our brightest blazes of gladness are commonly kindled by unexpected sparks.
—SAMUEL JOHNSON, lexicographer (1709–1784)

bibliotaph (BIB-lee-uh-taf) also **bibliotaphe**

noun   One who hoards books.

From Greek *biblio-* (book) + *taphos* (burial).

● His coworkers knew that Dostovich was a *bibliotaph,* but they were positively worried when he arranged to have half his paycheck directly deposited with the local bookstore.

> **Augustin's Principle**
> One reads books in an arithmetic progression but one buys in geometrical progression.
> —*Agustin F. Correa, Argentina*

biblioklept (BIB-lee-uh-klept)

noun   One who steals books.

From Greek *biblio-* (book) + *klept* (thief).

● A recent survey of public libraries revealed that among the books most often stolen, the top three are *The Joy of Sex* and its sequels, G.E.D. examination books, and *The Prophecies of Nostradamus.* Can you imagine a composite of a typical *biblioklept?*

> **Bluetooth and Love of His Folks for Books**
> When the Vikings were raiding England, frequently they'd pillage books from monasteries and hold them hostage. Of course, books were a lot more valuable back then.
> —*Loraine Earl, Canada*

• • •

Practice no vice because it's trivial.
Neglect no virtue because it's so.
—CHINESE PROVERB

Finally, at the other end of spectrum, here is a word for someone who doesn't exactly share this passion for books.

bibliophobe (BIB-lee-uh-foab)
noun   A book hater.
From *biblio-* (book) + *-phobe* (one who fears).

● Elia wasn't exactly a *bibliophobe,* but seeing books mostly on Princess Diana, weight loss, and Nostradamus in the local bookstore, she wondered if she cared about books at all.

●　●　●
Hitch your wagon to a star.
—RALPH WALDO EMERSON, philosopher and author (1803–1882)

CHAPTER 55

Mondegreens and Other Linguistic Faux Pas

Face it—you have been guilty of it since early childhood. Beginning with the nursery rhymes you heard on the playground, to the national anthem you recited in school to crooning with the love songs on the radio, you have been misinterpreting and repeating them. Now you know there is a word for it and that you are not alone. Luckily there is no Mondegreen Police. No matter what your native tongue, chances are you have experienced mondegreens in your language.

Whether you consider mondegreens a case of aural dyslexia or a variant of a Freudian slip, the results are often much more fascinating than the original matter. The mondegreen effect is not limited to lyrics either. More than one school librarian has seen distraught pupils complaining of not being able to locate the book mentioned in their class: Charles Darwin's seminal work, "Oranges and Peaches."

So how did we come to call this oral-cum-aural phenomenon *mondegreen?* It all started when a courageous woman named Sylvia Wright confessed to mishearing the following words of a Scottish folksong:

They hae slain the Earl of Moray / And laid him on the green

as

They hae slain the Earl Amurray / And Lady Mondegreen

Imagine Wright's disappointment when she discovered that there was no Lady Mondegreen who valiantly gave her life to be with her love. She wrote her story in the November 1954 issue of *Harper's Magazine,* and ever since we have labeled these occurrences in honor of Lady Mondegreen's sacrifice. Here are mondegreens and a few other words about words.

mondegreen (MON-di-green)
noun   A word or phrase resulting from mishearing a word or phrase.

● From their Pledge of Allegiance that begins with "I led the pigeons to the flag" to the warning that the school's "Super-Nintendo" ("superintendent") is coming for inspection, kids are one of the best sources of *mondegreens.*

No More Burnt Toast, Please!
A few months ago my five-year-old son informed us that he thought he was "black toast intolerant" (lactose intolerant).
   —*Michael Brunelle, Charlottesville, Virginia.*

• • •

The more we live by our intellect,
the less we understand the meaning of life.
—LEO TOLSTOY, author (1828–1910)

A Toyota

From my four-year-old son: That's not a toy ota, it's a big ota.

—Trina Bouvet, Sassenage, France

Diary, Uh!

There was a little girl who wrote home from summer camp, explaining that she had developed "dire rear."

—Daniel F. Harrison, Framington Hills, Michigan

Songful or Sinful?

The Sunday school treat involved a trip out, much eating, and the singing of hymns during the return journey. The children happily sang, "We can sing, full though we be," rather subverting the original "Weak and sinful though we be."

—Peter Collingwood, Colchester, United Kingdom

Toes, Too, Have an Aroma

After returning from the podiatrist, I told my husband I had a neuroma (a damaged nerve between the toes). My husband replied, "I could have told you your toes have an aroma."

—Tamara H. Thomas, Salt Lake City, Utah

• • •

As a well spent day brings happy sleep, so life well used brings happy death.
—LEONARDO DA VINCI, painter, engineer, and scientist (1452–1519)

Life after Death

Years ago, when my children were small and we were leaving for an out-of-town trip, my babysitter's father was supposed to come to the house to pick up the spare key for her. We had never met him before. Around dinnertime, when the doorbell rang, I opened the door and found a clergyman standing there who said, "A man's dead." While I was processing this, I gave him, I'm sure, one of my blankest "what are you talking about" looks. He repeated himself. When it dawned on me, I was embarrassed and went to get him the key. What he had actually said was, "I'm Anne's dad."

—*Susan Frank, Rockledge, Florida*

Heron, My Love

Television and radio commercials are wonderful providers of mondegreens. My particular favorite was a vacuum cleaner that promised to pick up all of my "pet heron dirt." As an avid birdwatcher, I would love to have a great blue heron as a pet, but I imagine they do make a horrible mess. After listening more closely, however, I learned that this sweeper actually picks up "pet hair and dirt." Alas, no pet heron for me.

—*Barbara Kirby, Dallas, Texas*

The Taste of Ultimate Convenience

Of course, there's always the company that offers "the ultimate inconvenience." I've heard this in radio ads not once, but twice!

—*Vicki Blier, Lexington, Massachusetts*

• • •

Never cut what you can untie.
—JOSEPH JOUBERT, essayist (1754–1824)

spoonerism (SPOO-nuh-riz-em)

noun   The transposition of usually initial sounds of words, producing a humorous result.

Spoonerisms have perhaps been around ever since we humans began feeling disconcerted, and as a result mismatched the sounds of two words, but the name for this affliction came to the English language only around a century ago. William Archibald Spooner (1844–1930), British clergyman and educator, was undoubtedly the finest practitioner of the art of spoonerism. And both of his professions gave him ample opportunity to unwittingly show his specialty. Some of the choicest examples from this eponymous man are:

- Addressing a truant student: "You have tasted two whole worms, you have hissed all my mystery lectures. You will leave by the next town drain."

- Toasting the queen: "Three cheers for our queer old dean!"

- Scolding a pyromaniac miscreant: "You have been caught fighting a liar in the quad."

- Officiating at a wedding: "It is now kisstomary to cuss the bride."

- Enquiring of the secretary of his university official: "Is the bean dizzy?"

- To another parishioner in a church: "I believe you're occu-pewing my pie. May I sew you to another sheet?"

Reverend Spooner, the father of spoonerisms, not only gave the English language a new word, an eponym, but also an artful device for repartee. The story goes that a member of Parliament cut off another by calling him a shining wit, and then apologized for making a spoonerism.

• • •

That sorrow which is the harbinger of joy is preferable
to the joy which is followed by sorrow.
—SAADI, poet (c. 1213–1291)

Cleaning the Government
One of my favorites, blurted out by the announcer who had the honor of introducing the first radio address by a president of the United States, is "Ladies and gentlemen, it is my very great pleasure to present the president of the United States, Mr. Hoobert Heever!"
—*Katherine E. Hudson, Grass Valley, California*

Say Cheese
As a dinner was coming to a close I once invited everyone to "Please chatter" upon arrival of the cheese platter!
—*Philippe Gray-Grzeszkiewicz, Sydney, Australia*

malapropism (MAL-uh-prop-iz-ehm)
noun   The humorous misuse of a word by confusing it with a similar-sounding word.
From Mrs. Malaprop, a character in Richard Sheridan's play *The Rivals* (1775), who confused words this way. She would refer someone as a "pineapple of perfection." At another time, she talked about "an allegory on the banks of the Nile." While she is a fictitious character, there are plenty of real-life folks who would fit in her shoes, and not all of them are women.

• • •

The man who is a pessimist before forty-eight knows too much; if he is an optimist after it, he knows too little.
—MARK TWAIN, author and humorist (1835–1910)

With Compliments

I was invited to some affair which required a black tie, so I dressed in same and was walking through the kitchen, headed for the garage. Our housekeeper took a look at me and said, "Oh, you look so extinguished." All I could say was, "Thank you."

—*Brian A. Fahey, Buffalo, New York*

Double Whammy

After uttering a characteristically malapropish phrase and having it brought to her attention, my mother said, "Well, just call me Mrs. Maladroit!"

—*John S. Fullford, Andover, MA*

Incompetence

This word reminds me of *The Rugrats* on Nickelodeon. I am usually recruited by my four-year-old to watch such things. This particular show uses malapropisms quite regularly, probably in an attempt to entertain the adults who watch. In one episode, for instance, Angelica, a four-year-old character on the show, sues her parents for making her eat broccoli. She subsequently fires her attorney for "gross incontinence."

—*Todd Hynson, Dallas, Texas*

• • •

The man who is denied the opportunity of taking decisions of importance begins to regard as important the decisions he is allowed to take.
—C. NORTHCOTE PARKINSON, author and historian (1909–1993)

Noah's Ark
A friend who unfortunately had a terrible flood in her basement wrote, "It was terrible! Water was flowing from every orpheus imaginable!"

—*Lisette J. Brodey, Fluortown, Pennsylvania*

With Love from Mother-in-Law
My dear ninety-four-year-old Cockney ma-in-law mangles the English language; we collect some of the more memorable comments. Here are some.

"My son's left BBC but he still does some work for them; he's semi-retarded."

"She loves those two boys; she just devours them."

"My mum sang in the choir until she was ninety and I fell into her footsteps."

"I plucked these shells from the Indian Ocean."

—*Shelagh Nation, Aurora, South Africa*

Shrinkage
Lots of chances for fans of *The Sopranos* to hear malapropisms—latest case in point: "There's no stigmata connected with going to a shrink."

—*Jill Henaghen, Tarpon Springs, Florida*

• • •

Pessimist: One who, when he has the choice of two evils, chooses both.
—OSCAR WILDE, playwright, author, and poet (1854–1900)

Dinner with God

A good friend of mine told me once that he and his wife were having dinner with some friends, and the subject turned to religion. At one point, his wife asked someone, "What religion are you afflicted with?"

—*Amy Turek, Lincoln, Nebraska*

Dig It

I once taught in a school where the principal was almost as famous as Norm Crosby. My personal favorite was broadcast over the intercom system after completing a successful fire drill. "Congratulations, students, you excavated the building in three minutes." I still have a vision of all those seventh and eighth graders outside with shovels digging their little hearts out.

—*Martha W. Sutton, Valdosta, Georgia*

• • •

Those who will not reason, are bigots, those who cannot, are fools, and those who dare not, are slaves.
—LORD BYRON, poet (1788–1824)

Answers to the "Discover the Theme" Chapters

Chapter 7. *Discover the Theme I:*
All of the words can be typed on a standard QWERTY keyboard using only one hand—either left or right. Try it. Here are some other words that fall in this category:

Left hand only: *abstract, reverberate*

Right hand only: *lollipop, lollop, minikin, minimum, opinion*

Chapter 30. *Discover the Theme II:*
All of the words have letters in alphabetical order. Here are some tidbits about words with this characteristic:

About 0.3 percent of the words in the English language have this property.

The longest words (seven characters) with this characteristic are *beefily* and *billowy*.

The first and last words showing this quality are *aa* (solidified lava) and *tux*.

The longest word (nine characters) with letters in reverse order is *spoonfeed*.

The first and last words with letters in reverse order are *baa* and *zymic*.

Chapter 43. Discover the Theme III:

All of the words have letters in reverse alphabetical order.

Bibliography

The universe in alphabetical order," novelist Anatole France once said of the dictionary. Open an unabridged dictionary and you are in a universe that is enjoyable, engrossing, and edifying. Here is a listing of some books and dictionaries you might find useful in your exploration in this universe.

Simpson, John A., and Edmund S. Weiner (eds). *The Oxford English Dictionary,* 2nd ed. New York: Oxford University Press, 1989. ISBN: 0-19-861186-2 (20-volume set).

It is also available in CD-ROM, as a single-volume edition with small print and a magnifying glass, and as a web subscription.

Bryson, Bill. *The Mother Tongue: English & How It Got That Way.* New York: Avon Books, 1996. ISBN: 0-380-71543-0.

A delightful read about the wonders of the language. The author's enthusiasm for the language is infectious.

McArthur, Tom. *The Oxford Companion to the English Language.* New York: Oxford University Press, 1992. ISBN: 0-19-214183-X.

A rich mine of almost everything one needs to know about the English language.

Bowler, Peter. *The Superior Person's Book of Words.* Boston: David R. Godine, 1998. ISBN: 0-87923-556-X.

The Superior Person series is a small collection of unusual and whimsical words collected and commented upon with a touch of irreverence.

Bowler, Peter. *The Superior Person's Second Book of Weird and Wondrous Words.* Boston: David R. Godine, 1992. ISBN: 0-87923-928-X.

Byrne, Josefa Heifetz. *Mrs. Byrne's Dictionary of Unusual, Obscure, and Preposterous Words.* New York: Citadel Press Book, 2000. ISBN: 0-8065-0498-6.

The more preposterous the word is, the better the chances you'll find it in this book.

Index of Words